GOD SPEAKS WE LISTEN

A hermeneutic journey through the scriptures for spiritual growth and effective application

Rev. Jackie Nelson

WRITEHOUSE PUBLISHING
Washington, DC

© 2016 – Rev. Jackie Nelson / www.fullcircle202.com

Published by WRITEHOUSE PUBLISHING
Washington, DC 20004

Printed in the United States of America

ISBN-13: 978-0998372037
ISBN-10: 099837203X

Scripture Bibliography provided in chapter lessons.

Cover Design: WHP/Alvario Languao

GOD

"I AM THE VINE, YE ARE THE BRANCHES. HE THAT ABIDETH IN ME, AND I IN HIM, THE SAME BRINGETH FORTH MUCH FRUIT: FOR WITHOUT ME YE CAN DO NOTHING." JOHN 15:5

REV. JACKIE NELSON
FULL CIRCLE MINISTRIES

DEDICATION

This book is dedicated to all those who hunger and thirst after righteousness; to fulfill the will of God for their lives and passionately endeavor to win souls for the Kingdom.

ACKNOWLEDGEMENTS

God my Father, Jesus my Savior, the Holy Spirit my Empowerment

---

Rev. Willie F. & Rev. Mary L. Wilson
E.M. Bounds
Dr. Bruce Wilkinson
Dr. Myles Monroe
Rev. Dr. Renita Weems
Rev. Dr. Claudette Copeland
Alfred P. Gibbs

My daughters:
Pastor Charlene R. Nelson-Scott (Dale)
Evang. Charrisse D. Nelson-McIntosh (Timothy)

My son:
P. Neal Nelson, Jr.

My grandchildren:
E'manuel M. McIntosh / Zari~Alexandria C. McIntosh

WriteHouse Publishing Co.

FOREWORD

⚬⚬⚬

God always speaks to us from the time He sought Adam in the Garden of Eden: *"Adam, where are you?"* to even our own darkest hour in the Valley of the Shadow of Death. God speaks. We need to listen. It is the very nature of God, the Creator, to be in constant communication with His creation. You may ask yourself, as the psalmist did, *"What is man that Thou art mindful of him?"*

The answer is simple; you are a Child of the Most High God. You have royal blood flowing through your veins. You are the apple of God's eye! The fact that you have picked up this revelatory book of sermons written and fervently preached by Rev. Jackie Nelson says that you have a clear understanding that God has a blessing with your name on it. If you pay close attention, you can claim it! It's yours!

Psalm 85:8-9 says:

> I can't wait to hear what he'll say.
> God's about to pronounce his people well,
> The holy people he loves so much,
> so they'll never again live like fools.
> See how close his salvation is to those who fear him?
> Our country is home base for Glory!   **The Message** (MSG)

Rev. Jackie Nelson is God's spectacular trumpet; a clearer voice on the Word of God, you will not hear. As long as I have known her, for over 25 years, she has honestly and most assuredly proclaimed the Gospel of Jesus Christ. As an associate minister at Union Temple Baptist Church in Washington, DC for many more years, Rev. Nelson has sung from the depths of her soul, praising God and preaching from the depths of her heart. Her Bible-based theology is rooted in the Good News of the Gospel. She has been, and continues to be, a phenomenal instrument of God's will…for His glory!

I have walked with Rev. Jackie in good times and in bad times. What I have come to learn is that she gives God praise each and every time. As you take this journey with Rev. Jackie, you, too, will experience beauty for ashes, joy for mourning and a 'Hallelujah anyhow, radical, peace beyond all understanding' kind of praise. In other words, when God speaks, we ought to listen.

I have also come to understand as she and I have been known to say, "Iron sharpens iron." Here's the key: Rev. Jackie is going to give you *the unvarnished truth* – so, that the people of God will no longer live like fools. Dr. Dennis Kimbro, author of *'What Makes the Great Great'* says, "When wealth is lost, nothing is lost; when health is lost, *something* is lost. But when integrity is lost, *all* is lost!" Rev. Nelson abides by this principle that when you remain true to integrity, you are in agreement with our Father. When you preach with integrity, you are aligned with forces of the universe and nothing can overtake you. When you stand, flat-footed and preach the Good News with integrity, you walk with Almighty God.

Rev. Jackie Nelson is surely preaching!

God is certainly speaking!

Are you really listening?

Rev. Adama M. Zawadi

Rev. Adama Melitte Zawadi
Founder & Co-Pastor of Akoma Redemption Ministries
Atlanta, Georgia

TABLE OF CONTENTS

LESSON 1

※

I WON'T TURN BACK

LESSON 1

"I WON'T TURN BACK"

In the book of St. Luke 9:62, Jesus stresses a point that does not speak to the reality of our human experience. It appears that His only concern is His own agenda with no regard as to what we are affected by and the cultural motifs that govern our response to a given situation.

Without clear consideration concerning the choices and decisions we make as it relates to our day-to-day which includes a plethora of circumstances: we can be left in limbo and teeter on the edge. The art of making a concrete choice or decision is the ability to weigh one's options as to what is required to accomplish a productive outcome.

How does one do this? By having a premise to build upon that will cause you to stay focused on the ultimate goal and not waiver due to the onslaught of any distractions. The objective of this lesson is the "CALL for FOCUSED and DETERMINED DISCIPLES" that are passionate about being a vessel of honor, fit to be used by God; thereby, resolving in their heart that "I Won't Turn Back."

A. The Declaration [a positive or formal statement]:

"I WON'T TURN BACK"

B. The Consideration [something that is kept in mind when making a decision]:

"TALK IS CHEAP, ACTIONS SPEAK LOUDER THAN WORDS"

3

C. The Actualization [turns into action or a fact]:

"ACTIONS FOLLOW WORDS"

D. The Disclosure [to make known]:

SCRIPTURE: **St. Luke 9:62**

(**KJV, RSV, NLT**) – Jesus said to him, no one having put his hand to the plow, and looks back, '**is fit**' for the Kingdom of God.

(**NIV**) – Jesus replied, no one who puts his hand to the plow and looks back '**is fit for service**' in the Kingdom of God.

(**GNB**) – Jesus said to him. Anyone who starts to plow and then keeps looking back '**is of no use**' for the Kingdom of God.

(**TMB**) – Jesus said, No procrastination, no backward looks, **you can't put God's Kingdom off till tomorrow, Seize the day.**

(**LAB for Students**) – Jesus said to him. Anyone who lets himself be distracted from the work I plan for him '**is not fit**' for the Kingdom of God.

(**TAB**) – Jesus said, **No one who puts his hand to the plow and looks back [to the things behind] is fit for the Kingdom of God.**

E. The Presentation [A message set forth for listeners to receive]:

The Cost of Discipleship and the Hindrances to Discipleship

The 3 would be followers of Jesus Christ:

Verse 57: The 1st one came with a lofty enthusiastic promise.

I will follow you wherever you go. Jesus asked him if he could handle His rejection (foxes have holes, birds have nest, but the son of man has nowhere to lay his head).

Explicitly, this contrasts the security of the son of man with the conditions of animals at the mercy of nature. Even animals, at the end of the day, have a place to call home. The son of man does not have that refuge or designated space

Implicitly, this saying of Jesus works on the assumption that the follower will be like the one who is followed.

Verse 59: The 2nd follower was directly called by Jesus. He would follow Jesus but asked for permission to go bury his father.

Note: The Jews were bound by custom to bury the dead, but Jesus knew that the man was suggesting that he would like to go home and care for his father until his death. To put off serving Jesus until there was a more convenient time in his busy life.

Jesus' harsh response to this follower was, let the dead bury the dead. **What did Jesus mean by this response?** He wanted the man to know that the priority of service to the Kingdom is to be set above every other priority; your business is not more important than the Father's business.

Note: Those who have not responded to the call to the Kingdom are like the dead. Those who have responded to

STUDY NOTES

the call to (Discipleship) are no longer dead. Their concern should be with life and the living.

Verses 61-62: The 3rd follower offers to follow Jesus. But he wants to say farewell to his family first. Jesus rebukes him, emphasizing again the unconditional demand of 'The Call to Discipleship.' To have one's hand on the plow and look back, was to have reservations about discipleship, thus making one not fit for the Kingdom of God.

Note: Fit for the Kingdom of God does not refer to salvation but to service. It's not at all a question of entrance into the Kingdom but of service in the Kingdom after entering it.

Note: No man, having put his hand to the plow, will look back, or look behind him for then he makes "balks" (hesitates) with his plow; and the ground he plows is not fit to be sown. A plow-man must produce a straight furrow (a narrow trench made in the ground by a plow). He must stay focused. The task of plowing requires a man's uninterrupted attention. Should he deviate in anyway, he becomes a sower not fit to scatter good seed for the kingdom of God.

Plowing is in order prior to Sowing. [Plow – to undertake with eagerness and vigor; to move or progress with driving force].

Remember, you are not fit for the job of kingdom building if you don't know how to break up fallow ground (uncultivated or inactive) . Once you have put your hand to the plow; don't allow challenging circumstances to cause you to look back or think about quitting. Looking back inclines

6

to drawing back and drawing back is to "Perdition"; hell, losing your soul to eternal damnation.

F. The Clarification [to make plain, clear or explain]:

The man Jesus and the works of his ministry inspired a lot of people. So much so that some of the people wanted to be a part of it. Jesus knew the magnitude of the task set before him and he understood that part of his mission was not to do it all by himself so he handpicked some followers with the sole purpose of creating disciples.

What was the voluntary desire to follow Jesus and the personal direct call to follow Jesus all about? It was the opportunity for one to become a disciple and embrace the privilege of discipleship.

This poses two questions:

1. **What is a Disciple?** A disciple is one who embraces and assists in spreading the teachings of another and imitates their practices (St. Luke 6:40): which is inclusive of the following:

    - Student – a person who is studying.

    - Learner – one who gains knowledge.

    - Follower – adherent devotee. [A Follower of Jesus Christ believes his doctrine, rest on his sacrifice, imbibes his spirit and imitates his example]

    - Apprentice – a person learning a trade by being employed or engaged in it.

2. **What is Discipleship?** The commitment to live as a disciple of Jesus Christ. Discipleship is a process that includes the following:

- Learning Bible truth.

- Applying the Bible truth to everyday life.

- Becoming like Christ.

- Sharing the teachings of Jesus with others.

- Serving the church.

- Fulfilling the goals God has personally designed for each person (St. Matthew 28:19-20- The Great Commission).

One's response to the clarion call to serve, be it voluntary or a personal direct call from God, is to be a disciple and engage in discipleship. This is God's way of letting us know that he needs us; we are the vessels through which God works. "I must work the works of him who sent me, while it is day: the night cometh, when no man can work" John 9:4.

That need, can only be fulfilled when we say "YES" with no hesitation to be God's representation here on the earth. Be a disciple that will stand up and fight against every antagonistic force that opposes God and his work in the reconciliation of Mankind.

G. The Resignation [a willful submission]:

Once you understand what a disciple is and what discipleship entails; there is another component of Discipleship. If you are adamant in your Declaration – "I WON'T TURN BACK": as you forge ahead, it is vital that you are well versed on the "CONDITIONS OF DISCIPLESHIP" which stress three essential elements.

The Conditions of Discipleship is found in St. Luke 9:23, If anyone would come after me (want to be my follower), let him deny himself (must put aside your selfish ambitions, put aside his own desires and conveniences) and take up his cross daily, and follow me (keep close to him).

Note: To deny one's self means a little more than face the dangers of our Christian calling, making sacrifices, giving up particular interests or possessions. IT IS A DEMAND FOR A <u>RADICAL</u> (forming a basis, going to the root of the matter) <u>REORIENTATION</u> (a necessary adjustment) OF LIFE – WITH SELF NO LONGER THE CENTER. <u>THE WILL OF GOD</u> MUST TAKE THE PLACE OF OUR OWN WILLS.

HOW DOES ONE KNOW WHAT GOD'S WILL IS?

By reading and studying The Bible intensely, this will enable you to habitually conform your thinking and behavior to God's word over a lifetime. As you read and study the Bible on a regular basis, your mind is renewed with a new way of thinking about life. This new-found mindset toward the "Word of God" will usher you into an ongoing "Fellowship" with God:

Thus, you will be equipped to make decisions with a biblically informed way of thinking (Psalm 119:15-16).

- **Note:** Take up his cross means to be willing and ready to lay down one's life just as Jesus did. (St. Matthew 10:38, He who does not take his cross and follow after Me is not worthy of Me.)

For one to be in compliance with St. Luke 9:23, as it relates to The Resignation you must be:

- **<u>DEVOTED</u>** – have a faithful heart with true purpose and earnest allegiance.

  1. Deuteronomy 6:5

  2. Psalm 119:38

  3. Psalm 31:23a

  4. Revelation 2:10

- **<u>DEDICATED</u>** – wholly committed to something

  Commitment demands a choice as well as demanding an action. It is a lifetime venture requiring time, work, and determination. One's commitment to the ways of Christ helps to build our faith and develop character.

  1. Joshua 24:14

  2. Proverbs 16:3

  3. Romans 12:1-2*

H. The Resolution [the act of resolving or determining an action or course of action]:

The scripture declares in II Corinthians 5:17, Therefore if any man be in Christ, he is a new creature: old things are passed away; behold, all things are become new. "All things are become new" speaks to Process. The old way of living is challenged with a new conviction to do the right thing and the new man yearns for the way and the things of God. Again, this speaks to Process. How does one stay on a steady course and not falter through this new process? There are two key elements that will under gird (to give fundamental support; to strengthen and secure) you as you experience this newness of life; they are Discipline and Perseverance.

- **DISCIPLINE** – character, obedience.

  Spiritual discipline is essential for Christian growth and development. It is a continual process that helps the believer mature in Christ and know God's will. It is also essential to deliverance from the power of sin and obedience to God's will.

  1. Deuteronomy 10:12-13

  2. St. John 14:15

  3. Galatians 5:22-23

  4. Colossians 3:12-16

  5. II Peter 1:5-8

- **PERSEVERANCE** – steady persistence in a course of action; a purposed activity maintained in spite of difficulties. A steadfast and long continued application.

  The attitude of Perseverance will enable you to faithfully endure and remain steadfast in the face of opposition, attack, and discouragement

  Perseverance involves patience- the ability to endure without complaint and with calmness (James 1:2-4). Perseverance also includes persistence in accomplishing goals and permanence for a lifetime of commitment (II Peter 1:5-8). As followers of Christ, we are to persevere in the following ways:

1. In Prayer (Ephesians 6:18)

2. In Faith (Hebrews 12:1-2)

3. In Obedience (Revelations 14:12)

4. In Service (I Corinthians 15:58)

5. In Spiritual Warfare (Ephesians 6:10-17)

I. **The Finalization** [a conclusion]

This lesson has dealt with three important factors as it pertains to our desire to follow Jesus; whether it is voluntarily or a direct personal response to his call to follow him. They are The Cost of Discipleship, The Hindrances to Discipleship, and The Conditions of Discipleship. Once we are abreast to the former, we must be cognizant of the ultimate objective in following Jesus Christ: God's Kingdom must be first.

The text makes it vividly clear that God does not want a half-hearted commitment from us; but a total surrender and submission to his will for our lives: as it relates to our being an uncompromised Disciple. Let it be our heartfelt motive to move ahead as builders/workers of the Kingdom without looking back. Christ must remain in our hearts without a rival (competing opposition or antagonist) (Romans 8:35-38).

We must share the Word of God with others because it is infinitely of greater importance than our worldly responsibilities and challenges. Should there ever be a conflict between the two; there should be no moments of hesitation ---- GOD FIRST ALWAYS!!!!!!!!!!!!!!!!!!

So, let it be written, so let it be done:

KJV: II Timothy 2:21 – If a man purge himself from these, he shall be a vessel of honor, sanctified, and meet for the master's use (to be of service to the Lord), and prepare unto every good work.

The Amplified Bible: II Timothy 2:21 – So whoever cleanses himself [from what is <u>ignoble</u> and unclean, who separates himself from content with contaminating and corrupting influences] will [then himself] be a vessel set apart and useful for honorable and noble purposes, consecrated and profitable to the master, fit and ready for any good work.

The Addendum:

OPERATING in the OVER-FLOW

When you are emphatic (definite) about your resolve: I WON'T TURN BACK"; and you have taken to heart everything it entails: you are now ready to operate in the "OVERFLOW". God can depend on you and you will have his stamp of approval regarding all that you do for his name sake.

What does the word "Operate" mean?

- Be in action

- Function

- Produce an effect

- Exert influence

What does the word "Over-flow" mean?

- Flow over (the brim, limits, etc.)

- To have boundless supply

- Extend beyond the limits

- Be very abundant

- To be filled in great measure

- Superfluous (more than enough)

What does it mean to "Operate in the Overflow?"

- To live a life of obedience so that your ear will be sensitized to the voice of God. When he speaks, you will listen, hear what he said, and respond willingly without provocation.

- To get filled that you will overflow, to produce an effect that provokes change so others can be recipients of your boundless supply. The ultimate objective is to pass it on!

- THE BOTTOM LINE is YOU ARE SOLD OUT! You are totally committed to a life of obedience and service to God.

GOD SPEAKS WE LISTEN

Study Notes

_____

_____

_____

_____

_____

_____

_____

_____

_____

_____

_____

_____

_____

_____

_____

_____

_____

_____

'God Speaks, We Listen: A hermeneutic journey through the scriptures for spiritual growth and effective application.'

GOD SPEAKS WE LISTEN

Study Notes

_____

_____

_____

_____

_____

_____

_____

_____

_____

_____

_____

_____

_____

_____

_____

_____

_____

_____

_____

'God Speaks, We Listen: A hermeneutic journey through the scriptures for spiritual growth and effective application.'

GOD SPEAKS WE LISTEN

Study Notes

_____

_____

_____

_____

_____

_____

_____

_____

_____

_____

_____

_____

_____

_____

_____

_____

_____

_____

_____

'God Speaks, We Listen: A hermeneutic journey through the scriptures for spiritual growth and effective application.'

GOD SPEAKS WE LISTEN

Study Notes

'God Speaks, We Listen: A hermeneutic journey through the scriptures for spiritual growth and effective application.'

GOD SPEAKS WE LISTEN
Study Notes

_____

_____

_____

_____

_____

_____

_____

_____

_____

_____

_____

_____

_____

_____

_____

_____

_____

'God Speaks, We Listen: A hermeneutic journey through the scriptures for spiritual growth and effective application.'

LESSON 2

THE ANTIDOTE FOR WHAT AILS YOU

LESSON 2

"THE ANTIDOTE FOR WHAT AILS YOU"

SCRIPTURE: **St. John 14:27**

TITLE: **The Antidote for What Ails You!!!!!!**

SUBJECT: **Peace of Mind**

PROPOSITION: I purpose to show the hearer that Jesus Christ gave us the gift of his inner peace so that we could be confident and assured that he is always with us as we encounter the onslaughts of life as well as being his witness here on earth.

OBJECTIVE: I want the hearer to know that peace of mind is the essential element to have if we are going to be productive instruments for the kingdom and live victorious lives.

(KJV, RSV, NLT) "Peace I leave with you, my peace I give unto you: not as the world giveth, give I unto you. Let not your heart be troubled, neither let it be afraid."

(NIV) "Peace I leave with you; my peace I give you. I do not give to you as the world gives. Do not let your hearts be troubled and do not be afraid."

(GNT) "Peace is what I leave with you; it is my own peace that I give you. I do not give it as the world does. Do not be worried and upset; do not be afraid."

23

STUDY NOTES

(TMB) "Peace I leave with you; My peace I give unto you, not as the world giveth, give I unto you. Let not your heart be troubled, neither let it be afraid."

Jesus Christ wasn't talking to sinners; but to disciples. They were not disconnected, but in relationship with the Lord. He gives the gift of; "Peace" and tells them, <u>Let not your heart be troubled, neither let it be afraid</u>. Let's deal with the "b" portion of the scripture.

Why did Jesus Christ say "Let not your heart, etc.? Because he knew about us. What I have experienced and observed about those of us who declare to be saved, sanctified and filled with the Holy Ghost is, we allow our hearts to be troubled.

Some of us fail to acknowledge that in some of the areas of our lives we are jacked up; discombobulated; dysfunctional; fear grips us when the normal is altered; fear grips us when we have to tread in unfamiliar territory.

Jesus Christ relates to us on our terms as He encourages us!

Internally and emotionally we're uneasy (outside, looks like all is well but inside you are like a shaken up soda; when you take the cap off it explodes all over the place. You live on the edge – worried, upset and terrified; there are questions you want the answers to that you can't figure out).

Physical pretense (actor, can play any role, but won't be who you really are)

Fashionably/alive (you wear bright colors, gorgeous styles)

Spiritual fashion persona (disbelief, uncertainty, and darkness). You allow your human capacity to resolve issues; to take precedence over your spiritual knowledge reminding you that you're not in this thing called life alone, God is with you.

Why did Jesus Christ say my "Peace" I leave with you, my "Peace" I give not as the world gives? Jesus Christ understood that the disciple's lives would go on after he went back to the Father so He wanted to leave them with the means to grab life by the horns and live it.

What do you need to live life to its fullest? Do you need family, money, good health, education, good job, support system, home, car, the Lord, a good church to attend, vision, passion? All these are great but there is one thing you need so you can live life to its fullest! There's something you have to have: Let me interject, psychologist, social workers have large caseloads; people spend 100's of dollars trying to get it. Pharmaceutical companies make millions prescribing medication to help one to have it.

So, what do you need to live life to its fullest? PEACE OF MIND!

The Mind is the center of mental activity; it is the part of a human being that "Thinks", "Feels", and "Wills".

The Mind:

1. In your mind is your personality, intellect, innermost character, feelings, and inclinations.

2. As a man/woman thinks in their heart (mind) so are they (**Proverbs 23:4**).

STUDY NOTES

3. Guard your heart (mind) with all diligence for out of it are the issues of life

(Proverbs 4:23).

4. It is the seat of all your plans and ideas.

5. Things originate and come into being.

6. It is the battleground for all things concerning you.

"PEACE"

- Serenity, quietness of mind

- State of tranquility

- Freedom of the mind from disturbance, annoyance, distraction, terror, anger, and anxiety.

- Inner peace; it has nothing to do with the world and its outside circumstances or events.

HOW DO I GET PEACE? There are some external things that afford peaceful moments: such as nature, water, gardening, music, helping others, reading, walking, and exercising.

NOTE: But, there is a talking about an internal quietness that is timed released; it will be there whenever you need it.

NOTE: "Peace" refers to the sense of wholeness and well-being that comes from a right relationship with God. He is Lord and Saviour; recognize you can't make it without him; committed to live life of obedience; and enjoy His bountiful blessing.

NOTE: This gift of "Peace" does not mean we are exempt from conflict or trials (**John 16:33b** – (…in this world you shall have tribulation: but be of good cheer; I have overcome the world) but it does mean calmness and confidence in the midst of it. HIS "Peace" TRANSCENDS ALL LOGIC and RATIONALE. I have to admit that this is reassuring; sounds good - but I have a question.

HOW DO YOU MAINTAIN "Peace of mind"? Ps 34:14b and **I PET 3:11b** -- Seek "Peace' and Pursue – How is that accomplished?

A. **WORK YOUR FAITH!**

God given measure of Faith (start with little and it will grow) "FAITH" comes by hearing; hearing by the Word of God. It enters your mind by hearing it preached, taught, or read which enables you to understand the Bible. By the Word of God - you receive direct information and knowledge about God, Jesus Christ and the Holy Spirit. All that the Godhead is, and can do, is established in the Word of God.

- Who you are and whose you are is in the Word of God.

- All that you can and cannot do is in the Word of God.

- All that once was, is now, and is yet to be, is in the Word of God.

- All that God needs from you and needs you to do, is in the Word of God.

STUDY NOTES

- All the knowledge about the enemy of your soul (Satan) and the fact that he is a defeated foe is in the Word of God.

The Word of God is fail safe and full proof (the Word won't return unto Him void and will go where He sends it to accomplish what He pleases). When you receive the Word of God with a sincere heart and you are clear on how much you need him to work in your life; then "Fruit-fulness is the guaranteed by-product:

1. Lost/save/soul

2. Nurture you into spiritual maturity

3. Meeting the needs of His people

THE JUST SHALL LIVE BY "FAITH."

Without it, you are selling God short or putting Him in a box, thus you have made a disclaimer - GOD CAN'T DO IT!

"FAITH" is the mechanism you use to cause God to show off and work on your behalf --God is eagerly waiting to show you what He can do. Is there anything too hard for God? Ephesians 3:20 "Now unto him that is able to do exceeding abundantly above all that we ask or think, according to the power that worketh in us."

NOTE: Once you get that 'Faith' working then you must:

B. ACTIVATE YOUR TRUST!!

Isaiah 26:3 "Thou will keep you in <u>Perfect</u>", "<u>Peace</u>", etc.; "Perfect Peace" - nothing lacking, no defects. "…whose mind is stayed on Him" – Word of God must be read carefully and often, studied memorized and lived. "…because

He trusteth in thee" – believe him; put all your confidence in Him; totally rely on Him.

NOTE:

- Things heavy on your mind? Can you do anything about it? If so, do it. If not, don't stress.

- Trials, tribulations, and burdens - Don't let it overwhelm you. **Romans 5:1-5** "Therefore being justified by faith, we have peace with God through our Lord Jesus Christ by whom also we have access by faith into this grace wherein we stand, and rejoice in hope of the glory of God. And not only so, but we glory in tribulations also: knowing that tribulation worketh patience; And patience, experience; and experience, hope: And hope maketh not ashamed; because the love of God is shed abroad in our hearts by the Holy Ghost which is given unto us."

- Financially strained and drained -- Don't worry -- **Philippians 4:19**, "But my God shall supply all your need according to his riches in glory by Christ Jesus."

Proverbs 3:5-6 "Trust in the LORD WITH ALL THINE HEART; AND LEAN NOT UNTO THINE OWN UNDERSTANDING. In all thy ways acknowledge him, and he shall direct thy paths."

Trust - assured reliance on the strength of another. Guard your heart for out of it, flows the issues/life. **Philippians 4: 6-8** "Be careful for nothing; but in everything by prayer and supplication with thanksgiving let your requests be made known unto God. And the peace of God, which passeth all understanding, shall keep your hearts and

STUDY NOTES

minds through Christ Jesus. Finally, brethren, whatsoever things are true, whatsoever things are honest, whatsoever things are just, whatsoever things are pure, whatsoever things are lovely, whatsoever things are of good report; if there be any virtue, and if there be any praise, THINK ON THESE THINGS."

THIS PERFECT PEACE:

- Enable you to handle your business.

NOTE: When it appears to you that "God" is still, know that "God" is never still -- God describes himself as "I AM THAT I AM' He's a keeper, and protector.

- You can function in a dysfunctional atmosphere.

- You have a sincere smile on your face when you should be frowning.

- In the midst of the wars in your life, you can still fight although it looks like you are defeated.

- The forces of hell are puzzled because it hit you with its best shot and you are still standing.

- Causes you to be tenacious in holding on to "God's" promises.

- You live in expectation that "God" will do what he says he will do.

Work your Faith, activate your trust; then there is nothing else to do but:

C. ELEVATE YOUR PRAISE!

Remember that you know someone; you know something about that someone; you know what that someone is capable of; and that someone supersedes every human situation that has existed, exist, and yet to come into existence:

Who is this someone? -- EL ELYon – The Most High God

You must Practice – Patient and Persistent Praise:

- **Isaiah40:31** "But they that wait upon the LORD shall renew their strength; they shall mount up with wings as eagles; they shall run, and not be weary; and they shall walk, and not faint."

- **Psalms 34:1** "I will bless the Lord at all times: his praise shall continually be in my mouth."

- **Habakkuk 3:17-18** "Although the fig tree shall not blossom, neither shall fruit be in the vines; the labour of the olive shall fail, and the fields shall yield no meat; the flock shall be cut off from the fold, and there shall be no herd in the stalls: Yet I will rejoice in the LORD, I WILL JOY IN THE GOD OF MY SALVATION."

STUDY NOTES

GOD SPEAKS WE LISTEN
Study Notes

_____
_____
_____
_____
_____
_____
_____
_____
_____
_____
_____
_____
_____
_____
_____
_____
_____
_____
_____
_____
_____

'God Speaks, We Listen: A hermeneutic journey through the scriptures for spiritual growth and effective application.'

GOD SPEAKS WE LISTEN
Study Notes

_____

_____

_____

_____

_____

_____

_____

_____

_____

_____

_____

_____

_____

_____

_____

_____

_____

_____

_____

'God Speaks, We Listen: A hermeneutic journey through the scriptures for spiritual growth and effective application.'

GOD SPEAKS WE LISTEN

Study Notes

_____

_____

_____

_____

_____

_____

_____

_____

_____

_____

_____

_____

_____

_____

_____

_____

_____

_____

'God Speaks, We Listen: A hermeneutic journey through the scriptures for spiritual growth and effective application.'

GOD SPEAKS WE LISTEN

Study Notes

_____

_____

_____

_____

_____

_____

_____

_____

_____

_____

_____

_____

_____

_____

_____

_____

_____

_____

_____

_____

'God Speaks, We Listen: A hermeneutic journey through the scriptures for spiritual growth and effective application.'

GOD SPEAKS WE LISTEN

Study Notes

_____

_____

_____

_____

_____

_____

_____

_____

_____

_____

_____

_____

_____

_____

_____

_____

_____

_____

_____

_____

_____

'God Speaks, We Listen: A hermeneutic journey through the scriptures for spiritual growth and effective application.'

LESSON 3

THINGS WILL WORK FOR YOU

LESSON 3

"THINGS WILL WORK FOR YOU"

SCRIPTURE: **Psalms 34:15, 4, 19**

TITLE: **Things Will Work for Your Good, but You Must Be Worked!**

SUBJECT: **Things Will Work for Your Good, but You Must Be Worked!**

PROPOSITION: I purpose to show the hearer that God is working *for* them and He is also working *in* them to ensure that this divinely concerted effort solidifies one's faith to persevere with a grateful heart.

OBJECTIVE: I want the hearer to know that God makes us into the best that we can be as He catapults us into progressive dimensions of growth and victory.

Psalms 34:15, "The eyes of the LORD are upon the righteous, and his ears are open unto their cry."

Psalms 34:4, "I sought the LORD, and he heard me, and delivered me from all my fears."

Psalms 34:19, "Many are the afflictions of the righteous: but the LORD delivereth him out of them all."

NOTE: Forrest Gump/Mom – Life is like a box of chocolates, you never know what you are going to get.

STUDY NOTES

The unpredictability of life - when you think you're prepared, you're not. When you think you're not prepared, you are. Then there are times when things happen in life that totally take you by surprise. Some of us will rise to the occasion; while others of us will find ourselves drowning; about to go under for the 3rd time; or we are maintaining while bewitched, bothered, and bewildered. The inevitable effect of life's encounters make you wonder; what caused this to happen and why does it affect me like this? We become analytical, investigative, trying to get some kind of resolve. I would love to be in heaven, as the master of my fate or the captain at the helm or better yet the omnipresent, omniscient, omnipotent one in charge. But then I, the created one would be attempting to usurp the authority of the Creator: and GOD IS NOT HAVING THAT!

So, as we sojourn through life it would help us tremendously if we understood that the stage is set, the journey is mapped out; and your destiny is decided. Jeremiah 29:11, "For I know the thoughts that I think toward you, saith the LORD, thoughts of peace, and not of evil, to give you an expected end."

NOTE: When you are destined for greatness:

- **Greatness is whatever is unique to you; no one else can do it or has it like you because it will be your tailored niche**
- **God will give you favor in the presence of your enemy**
- **Opposition will attempt to conjure up a strategy to break you down, spoil your success, and stop your progress**

EXERGESIS: The text speaks today

The Psalms, is the hymnbook of Israel and they are the windows into how the people of God honestly interact with Him in every kind of conceivable situation; teach us how to respond to God, train us how to talk to God. David, the author of 73 Psalms, was the youngest son of Jesse. He was a courageous shepherd boy chosen by God to be king of Israel. He was anointed by Samuel, sanction and appointed. A musician. He slew Goliath; gained favor with Saul. Excelled in warfare. The people praised him.

NOTE: David loved God. God was David's mainstay. God loved David. David was God's concern but this dynamic did not exempt David from the vicissitudes of life.

Saul was jealous of David and plotted many times to kill him. David was a fugitive running for his life. He went to the Philistine country of Gath where king Achish ruled. One of the king's servants recognize David. David feared for his life and acted as though he was a man insane. Achish dismissed him as insane. It was this event that motivated David to pen this Psalm, **Psalms 34:15a**, "The eyes of the Lord are upon the righteous…"

NOTE: God sees us righteous before we see ourselves that way because we come from Him (the essence of God is in us) His 'DNA' is in all of us.

The eyes of the Lord… and **Psalms 34:15b** continues, "… and His ears are open unto their cry."

NOTE: We need to look at afflictions, trouble, hardship, misery, misfortune, stress, and strain in a different way: it's only a test.

STUDY NOTES

Proverbs 17:3, "The fining pot is for silver, and the furnace for gold: but the LORD trieth the hearts."

Jeramiah 17:10, "I the LORD search the heart, I try the reins, even to give every man according to his ways, and according to the fruit of his doings."

Psalms 66:10-11, "For thou, O God, hast proved us: thou hast tried us, as silver is tried. Thou broughtest us into the net; thou laidst affliction upon our loins."

Isaiah 48:10, "Behold, I have refined thee, but not with silver; I have chosen thee in the furnace of affliction."

WHAT is the purpose for the TEST?

The test is to disclose:

- HOW YOU WILL REACT

- HOW YOU WILL RESPOND

- THE ATTITUDE YOU EMBRACE

- SHOW WHAT YOU ARE MADE OF

- IT WILL IDENTIFY WHAT YOU LACK

- HELP IDENTIFY WHAT YOU NEED

- WHETHER YOU ARE IN IT FOR THE LONG HAUL

- WILL YOU QUIT MID-STREAM

NOTE: DON'T DESPISE THE TEST!

- Can't get driver's license without passing the test

- Can't be a lawyer without passing the Bar

- Can't be a licensed social worker without passing the test

- Can't be a registered nurse without passing the test

Passing the test shows that you are CERTIFIED, BON-AFIDE and AUTHORIZED to FULFILL the TASK AT HAND.

NOTE: All the circumstances and situations we encounter in life are <u>designed with God's purpose in mind</u>.

What is God's purpose? To look out for you and extend His grace to you so that you will glorify His name.

NOTE: One's faithfulness to God as well as our desire to achieve our aspirations and accomplish our goals --- does not mean that we will have a carefree life, it's going to work for your good; BUT YOU MUST BE WORKED!

Example:

Every class is a challenge. You will find yourself saying, this class is working me. If God has anything to do with what's going on in your life right now you will learn how to handle the experiences of life and not let them handle you. In other words, *you will develop good coping skills.* My brother, sister, young ladies and gentlemen, **STUFF HAPPENS!** You may ask:

- How does one bare up in affliction?

- How do I keep my head when trouble over-whelms me?

- How do I maintain my sanity when the stress and strain makes me feel like I'm about to lose my mind?

STUDY NOTES

STUDY NOTES

Answer --- As God is working for your good; **LET HIM WORK YOU!**

A. PRAYER

Psalms 34:4, David said, "I sought the Lord in my distress, entreated his favor, asked His help and He heard me: answered my request and delivered me from all my fears."

What was David afraid of? He was afraid of literally dying coupled with the uneasiness and agitation produced by his fear.

The onset of trouble must be matched with the onset of Prayer. Prayer summons the God of deliverance to our aid.

It's at this time that God's Providence is working for us and his Grace is working in us.

> **PRAYER:**
>
> - Quick on your feet – you know where your help comes from
>
> - Seek God's counsel – follow His lead
>
> - Aggressive prayer warrior – have the key to loose and bind getting results and change
>
> - Outwit your circumstance – cleverly thinking it through gives you staying power

My brother, sister, young ladies and gentlemen, STUFF HAPPENS! As God is working for your good; LET HIM WORK YOU!

B. PERSEVERE

Psalms 34:19, "Many are the afflictions of the righteous: but the LORD delivereth him out of them all. (KJV)

Psalms 34:19, "The good man, (woman) suffers many troubles, but the Lord saves them from them all." (GNB)

David was surviving, running. God was with David; but all odds seem to be against him. His right now looked nothing like the things he was promised or desired. **(this poses a question)** -- What will we need to do so that we will not become a "Prisoner" to those things that overshadow any glimpse of hope? **(answer)** Don't let the cloudiness of your right now darken the sunlight of your yet to be!! David didn't let his circumstances confine his faith but it ignited his faith. And likewise, in order to remain steadfast in spite of those things that hinder us; we must learn to embrace the inescapable "PROCESS OF BECOMING" & Key Word is "PRESERVENCE!!!!

- Pregnant possibilities now birth anew, travailing to obtain it for it must come to pass; to toil, exert oneself

  Painfully difficult

  Burdensome work

  Suffering resulting/mental/physical

  Hardship

- I decree it, declare it, and call it in the spirit; to become what God designed me to be:

  o Shed some things – put on some new things

45

STUDY NOTES

- o Stop some things – start some new things

- o Endure some things – reassess some things

- o Separate from some things – reunite with some things

- o Embrace some things – eradicate some things

- o Accept some things – reject some things

- Like an Olive, pressed to get that pure oil

- Grapes pressed and aged to get the best wine

Your future, your promises shall be fulfilled. Yes, you shall obtain it for it must come to pass. David knew his right now looked nothing like it was going to be, 'King David'; I decree it, declare it, and call it in the spirit to "MANIFEST!"

C. PRAISE GOD

Don't start your day without gratitude; commit yourself to ceaseless praise.

DON'T YOU WORRY ABOUT A THING, BECAUSE EVERYTHING WILL BE ALRIGHT!

If God is who he says He is and can do what He says he can do (**Philippians 4:4** and **6-7**) vs-8 "…whatsoever things are true, honest, just, pure, lovely, are of good report, if there be any virtue, praise, think on these things."

No matter my state:

- Up or down

- Happy or sad

- Disappointed or gratified

- Stressed or blessed

- Whole or broken

- Whether I'm right, keep a level head (*God's grace is abounding upon me*) or wrong – You didn't cut me off (*Mercy pleaded my case*)

GOD DESERVES MY PRAISE!

Praise is comely for the upright - Praise is what we do.

God inhabits the praise of His people.

Praise Him in advance.

STUDY NOTES

GOD SPEAKS WE LISTEN

Study Notes

_____

_____

_____

_____

_____

_____

_____

_____

_____

_____

_____

_____

_____

_____

_____

_____

_____

_____

'God Speaks, We Listen: A hermeneutic journey through the scriptures for spiritual growth and effective application.'

GOD SPEAKS WE LISTEN

Study Notes

_____

_____

_____

_____

_____

_____

_____

_____

_____

_____

_____

_____

_____

_____

_____

_____

_____

_____

'God Speaks, We Listen: A hermeneutic journey through the scriptures for spiritual growth and effective application.'

GOD SPEAKS WE LISTEN

Study Notes

_____

_____

_____

_____

_____

_____

_____

_____

_____

_____

_____

_____

_____

_____

_____

_____

_____

_____

_____

'God Speaks, We Listen: A hermeneutic journey through the scriptures for spiritual growth and effective application.'

GOD SPEAKS WE LISTEN

Study Notes

_____

_____

_____

_____

_____

_____

_____

_____

_____

_____

_____

_____

_____

_____

_____

_____

_____

_____

_____

'God Speaks, We Listen: A hermeneutic journey through the scriptures for spiritual growth and effective application.'

GOD SPEAKS
WE LISTEN

Study Notes

_____

_____

_____

_____

_____

_____

_____

_____

_____

_____

_____

_____

_____

_____

_____

_____

_____

_____

_____

'God Speaks, We Listen: A hermeneutic journey through the scriptures for spiritual growth and effective application.'

LESSON 4

꩜

GOD IS MY SECURITY BLANKET

LESSON 4

"GOD IS MY SECURITY BLANKET"

SCRIPTURE: **Psalm 34:8**

TITLE: **God is My Security Blanket**

SUBJECT: **The Goodness of God will usher you into a safe place that will guarantee <u>the ultimate</u> (representing a limit beyond which further progress is impossible) <u>victory</u> (a success or superior position achieved against any opponent, opposition, difficulty, etc).**

PROPOSITION: I purpose to show the hearer the blessing they will experience as they personally discover God's goodness and seek Him as their refuge (a place of shelter, protection or safety).

OBJECTIVE: I want the hearer to **bask** (to feel secure under some benevolent influence) in God's goodness and be **confident** (strong belief of full assurance) that victory will always be the conclusion for whatever they go through in life.

Psalms 34:8 "O taste and see that the LORD is good: blessed is the man that trusteth in Him."

Book of Psalms, (Israel's Book of Hymns), Songs of Praise to God, David, the author, 8th son/Jesse, great grandson of Ruth and Boaz, shepherd boy (killed a lion and bear), anointed by the Prophet Samuel, Israel's next King, musician, armour bearer, killed Goliath, warrior, husband,

55

STUDY NOTES

father, fugitive, king, adulterer, murderer, and yet God called him a man after his own heart

David, wrote this Psalm when he was a fugitive/running from king Saul. (Saul was chosen as Israel's 1st king; became frustrated by his own mental torment for disappointing God, developed this intense hatred for David, whom the people elevated over him and he was afraid of David.) God was with David and departed from Saul. So, Saul purposed in his heart and his sole focus was to abort David's destiny of fulfilling God's appointment as the anointed chosen one; Israel's next king. Saul tried to kill David seven times. David was on the run always having to watch his back (**to be careful of the people around you, making certain that they do nothing to harm you**).

David **left Jerusalem** and decided to go to Gath (Goliath's hometown- Philistine country; they hated the Jews). He went to king Achish, the king's servants recognized David. David was in a **precarious** (exposed to, involving danger dependant on the will or pleasure of another) position, he was shaking in his sandals because of fear but **quick on his feet** (learned to think and act quickly); David pretended to be a mad man; crazy and king Achish dismissed him (in ancient times the world regarded the insane as being an evil sign. They were exempt from harm lest the gods become angry). David was able to get out of Gath alive and he wrote Psalms in homage (something done or given in acknowledgment or consideration of the worth of another) to God.

NOTE: David had a relationship with God; that relationship had many **experiences** (the encountering, or undergoing of things generally as they occur in the course of life); **and the outcome of those experiences <u>fortified</u>** (to support or confirm) **his <u>confidence</u>** (trustworthiness, or reliability of a person) **in God. David is so excited** that he wants to offer us an invitation to experience the same. "Oh, taste and see that the Lord is good!!!! Blessed is the man who takes refuge in Him."

Question #1

(1) Who is David talking about? "Taste and See that the Lord is good."

"Song - He is Lord"

He is Lord, He is Lord

He has risen from the dead

And He is Lord

Every knee shall bow

Every tongue confess

That Jesus Christ is Lord

I knew that Jesus Christ's time had not come yet: so, I researched the word Lord in Hebrew. The Orthodox Jews didn't utter the name YAHWEH because it was sacred, it was only used for writing and print. When they were in prayer, worship or discussion, the name Adonai was used (Hebrew for LORD). (When you see "Lord" in "OT" it is a replacement for God's Hebrew name "Yahweh")

Definition of Lord - a person who has authority, control, or power over others!

SOUNDS LIKE GOD TO ME!

STUDY NOTES

STUDY NOTES

Question #2

(2) What is he saying about God? That if you "Taste and See that the Lord is **Good" (having admirable, pleasing, superior, or positive qualities); you will find** out that YOU will be happy if you take refuge in Him.

NOTE: In a general sense "See" comes before the "Taste", (your favorite thing) (creativity, presentation, and taste) we make discoveries and have enjoyment; you will have an experience you can vouch for that can't be denied.

Question #3

(3) How can we take David up on his invitation and have it work for us? As it pertains to God, the "See" comes after the "Taste" - when you "Taste" you experience God's goodness; as a result of your "Taste", you will "See" - realize God's goodness and take comfort in it (He will be our refuge).

A. SEARCH GOD'S RECORD!

God is the master of goodness. Goodness is the essence of His nature; God's goodness refers to His gracious generosity in providing abundantly for our needs and showering us with many benefits.

Creation - God spoke where there was nothing and it came into existence. He created man from the dust of the earth and breathed His essence into him and said that's good.

Man's redemption – Jesus Christ became the propitiation (satisfaction) for our sins - to bridge the gap between mankind and Himself (the act of reconciliation)

Providing a 'Paraclete' (one called to the aide of another) The Holy Spirit - advocate; intercessor; regenerates us; sanctifies us; fills and empowers us; He's our comforter; teacher; keeper; convicts us of sin; guides us into all truth; produces in us fruit (Gal 5:22-23) which is evidence of His work and presence; seals us until the day of redemption; speaks to us and through us; knows the things of God; and bring things back to our remembrance.

He's so good that He inspired Man to write the BIBLE (that's His record): in it contains the **divine** answer to the deepest needs of humanity; sheds light on our path in a dark world; and sets forth the way to our eternal wellbeing.

God's goodness: Helps us in our actions (**be right, do right, act right**); presides over our intentions (**ensures our motives are pure**); inspects our different situations (**you are the person of interest; God has your best interest at heart**); He perpetually cares for us **(Isaiah 41:10)** and **(Hebrews 13:5**, "I'll never leave nor forsake you."

B. STAND SECURE IN GOD'S ABILITY!

God already knows how we're going to respond to the things that take place in our lives:

- In ready alert - we're taken back, feel the brunt of the event, can make a wise decision to get a grip on the situation before it gets a grip on us

- Function in slow motion - caught up in our feelings when things happen and experience this massive wave of frustration, betrayal, rejection, disappointment: with a victim mentality, woe is me

- Shut down - feel helpless, lost, and don't know what to do

GOD IS YOUR REFUGE! – "Blessed, happy is the man that takes refuge in Him!!!" **What does that mean?** You need a Power that's greater than what's coming at you or what you are going through to show up and fix it - This is what is called the act of self-abandonment and complete dependence upon another.

Psalms 34:6 "This poor man cried, and the LORD heard him, and saved him out of all his troubles."

Trouble and Prayer should be synonymous (*equally attended to*) meaning, trouble should never arise and you not immediately pray. Scriptures reiterate the importance of prayer: "Men ought to always pray, not faint; pray without ceasing; the effectual fervent prayer of the righteous avails much."

Prayer - recognizes God in the time of trouble; Prayer sees God's hand in trouble and prays about it. Prayer enables us to see wise results in trouble. Prayer in trouble drives us away from unbelief, saves us from doubt, and delivers us from all vain and foolish questionings because of our experience. **ALL THINGS ARE UNDER DIVINE CONTROL!**

NOTE: All the things we encounter, living this thing called life (be it good, bad, indifferent, self-inflicted, or put upon us); it's designed to remind you that *your circumstances don't change who God is: they just ignite what He does.* **Ephesians 3:20**, "Now unto Him that is able to do exceeding abundantly above all that we ask or think, according to the power that worketh in us."

If you know who I am; let me do what I do! God is say-ing, you need relief, a way made, door open/shut; moun-tain moved; things to change; take your hands off of it and let me put my hands on it; you get out of the way and let me clear the way because:

- o   I AM that I AM (active present reality)

- o   El El Yon (The most High God)

- o   Sovereign (In Control, I do what I want, When I want, How I want, Where I want)

- o   Omnipotent (All Powerful)

- o   Jehovah Nissi (my banner)

- o   Jehovah Shalom (my peace)

- o   Jehovah Rohi (my shepherd)

- o   Jehovah Rapha (my healer)

- o   Jehovah Jireh (my provider)

- o   El Shaddai (the almighty God - more than enough).

Philippians 4:19 "But my God shall supply all your need according to his riches in glory by Christ Jesus."

Isaiah 54:17, "No weapon that is formed against thee shall prosper; and every tongue that shall rise against thee in judgment thou shalt condemn. This is the heritage of the servants of the LORD, and their righteousness is of me, saith the LORD."

Philippians 1:6 "Being confident of this very thing, that he which hath begun a good work in you will perform it until the day of Jesus Christ:"

STUDY NOTES

Isaiah 43:1-2 "Lord saying, "But now thus saith the LORD that created thee, O Jacob, and he that formed thee, O Israel, Fear not: for I have redeemed thee, I have called thee by thy name; thou art mine. When thou passest through the waters, I will be with thee; and through the rivers, they shall not overflow thee: when thou walkest through the fire, thou shalt not be burned; neither shall the flame kindle upon thee."

YOU ARE PRECIOUS and HONORED IN GOD'S SIGHT -- HE LOVES YOU!

C. SELECT A <u>TESTIMONY</u> (DECLARATION OR STATEMENTOF OF FACT)

They overcame by the Blood of Lamb and the Word of their Testimony: **YOUR TESTIMONY IS THE CATALYST** (thing that precipitates change) **TO HERALD** (proclaim the approach of; usher in) you to **VICTORY** (a success or superior position achieved against any opponent, opposition, difficulty, etc.)!

- When I look back over my life and I think things over, all of my good days out weigh my bad days. I won't complain.

SAY WHAT YOU NEED TO SAY!

- I would have fainted, unless I had believed to see the goodness of the Lord in the land of the living.

- Through many dangers, toils, and snares, etc. t'was grace that brought me safe this far and grace will lead me on.

- The Song - I Won't Complain.

I've had some good days

I've had some hills to climb

I've had some weary days

And lonely nights

But when I look around

And I think things over

All of my good days

They outweigh my bad days

So, I won't complain

- **Psalms 34: 1-3,** "I will bless the LORD at all times: his praise shall continually be in my mouth. My soul shall make her boast in the LORD: the humble shall hear thereof, and be glad. O magnify the LORD with me, and let us exalt his name together."

GOD IS MY SECURITY BLANKET!

NOTE: Don't ever forget what God has done for you; brought you through; held on to you; fought for you; saved the day; made a way; showed up on time. Hold on, don't get weary, weeping may endure for a night, but joy!

GOD IS MY SECURITY BLANKET!

GOD SPEAKS WE LISTEN

Study Notes

'God Speaks, We Listen: A hermeneutic journey through the scriptures for spiritual growth and effective application.'

GOD SPEAKS WE LISTEN

Study Notes

_____

_____

_____

_____

_____

_____

_____

_____

_____

_____

_____

_____

_____

_____

_____

_____

_____

_____

_____

_____

'God Speaks, We Listen: A hermeneutic journey through the scriptures for spiritual growth and effective application.'

GOD SPEAKS WE LISTEN

Study Notes

_____

_____

_____

_____

_____

_____

_____

_____

_____

_____

_____

_____

_____

_____

_____

_____

_____

_____

_____

_____

'God Speaks, We Listen: A hermeneutic journey through the scriptures for spiritual growth and effective application.'

GOD SPEAKS WE LISTEN

Study Notes

_____

_____

_____

_____

_____

_____

_____

_____

_____

_____

_____

_____

_____

_____

_____

_____

_____

_____

'God Speaks, We Listen: A hermeneutic journey through the scriptures for spiritual growth and effective application.'

GOD SPEAKS WE LISTEN

Study Notes

_____

_____

_____

_____

_____

_____

_____

_____

_____

_____

_____

_____

_____

_____

_____

_____

_____

_____

'God Speaks, We Listen: A hermeneutic journey through the scriptures for spiritual growth and effective application.'

LESSON 5

USE WHAT YOU GOT TO YOU GET WHAT YOU WANT

LESSON 5

"USE WHAT YOU GOT TO GET WHAT YOU WANT!"

SCRIPTURE: **Ephesians 3:14-21 (Ephesians 3:20)**

TITLE: **Use What You Got to Get What You Want!**

SUBJECT: **You Are Powerful!**

PROPOSITION: I purpose to show the hearer that they have the power to evoke God to do phenomenal things.

OBJECTIVE: I want the hearer to know that God's abilities will be activated in their life if they utilize the Power they have within them.

In verses 1-13 of our scripture, Paul was in a Roman prison. Wrote a letter to the church at Ephesus. He's God's steward charged to reveal great truths to the New Testament church; it is a living organism united in Jesus Christ. Paul tells the believing Jews, that the believing Gentiles are fellow heirs, members, and partakers of God's promises. They are to enjoy equal title and privileges through their faith in Jesus Christ. The Gentiles were concerned about all that Paul was suffering for their cause but he told them not to sweat it; it was his honor to be used by God on their behalf.

In verses 14-19 Paul prays for them, US:

- Be strengthened with the power of His might – (spiritual aptitude to be mature, stable, intelligent Christians

71

- Jesus Christ dwells in our hearts by faith – Jesus Christ's characteristics will be the influence that drives our day to day existence

- Be rooted and grounded in love – be established in Love as a way of life, **I Corinthians 13:4-7**, "Charity suffereth long, and is kind; charity envieth not; charity vaunteth not itself, is not puffed up, Doth not behave itself unseemly, seeketh not her own, is not easily provoked, thinketh no evil; Rejoiceth not in iniquity, but rejoiceth in the truth; Beareth all things, believeth all things, hopeth all things, endureth all things."

- That all the saints will know how **long, wide, deep,** and **high** the love of Jesus Christ is and experience His love in a personal way

- The goal is for our lives to become the embodiment of God Himself

In verse 20, Paul closes in prayer with a great exultation of praise to God; yet he enlightens us!

NOTE: That prayer, Paul prayed could be quite mind-boggling.

NOTE: Don't take all that I have prayed about concerning you and see the limitations based on your human comprehension, human nature but look at the "POWER" of God. Paul is also saying – God can't do a thing for you if you don't know what you have working for you.

Ephesians 3:20. "Now unto him that is able to do exceeding abundantly above all that we ask or think, according to the power that worketh in us."

NOTE: God has endowed you with "POWER" to tap into all His resources as it applies to every facet of your life.

A. **YOU ARE POWERFUL!**

What makes you "Powerful?"

Four (4) things[i]:

1. **The Power of the Blood** – the shedding of blood reconciles us back to God; we have a Champion's "DNA" that gives us what we need to conquer a defeated foe.

2. **The Power of the Holy Spirit – Acts 1:8a**, "But ye shall receive power, after that the Holy Ghost is come upon you"; 3rd person/Trinity through whom God acts – Holy Spirit reveals God's will; empowers individuals; giver of **Mental Gifts** (reasoning ability, excellent memory, striking tenet for math, strong language skills) and **Spiritual Gifts (I Corinthians 12:8-10; Ephesians 4:7-13; Rom 12-3-8**) anoints us; seals us; helps us; teacher; guide; and intercessor.

3. **The Power of the Word** – shows you who God is; who you are; will inform you of the things you need to do and how to do them; gives us faith; it's a hammer, fire that breaks a rock; a sword; discerner of the heart; it transforms us; it builds character; the divine answer to the deepest needs of humanity; and it sets forth the way to our eternal wellbeing.

---

i R.A. Torrey – "How to Obtain Fullness of Power" 1982, 1984 by Whitaker House

4. **The Power of Prayer** – the effect of the Power of Prayer begins when you recognize your ineptness, frailties and helplessness without God and you become cognizant of the fact that 'TOTAL DEPENDENCE ON GOD IS NECESSARY.

NOTE: This is the type of Power that says you are someone to be reckoned with. You are Confident and Fortified!

NOTE: Knowing what you have speaks volumes to what you're capable of and what you have determines what you get. If you are powerful, then there is something you should know about yourself!

B. **YOU ARE A MOVER** and **A SHAKER!**

We are spiritual people but we live in a natural world. We must take that spirituality and wrap it around the natural: tend to the needs of everyone on all levels. We are to impact the world, not the world impact us. We are to impress the world not the world impress us.

In the natural goings on in the world, we are to make sure that God plays a vital role, (is all up in it). **The devil is making every attempt to kill the churches influence in the natural world by emphasizing its (extenuating ones) flaws and frailties. But the few of us that miss the mark do not outnumber those of us that are on the mark. Let's not forget that!**

NOTE: If the world is to see God, they have to see Him through something they can relate to, i.e., another God-filled human being. This has nothing to do with whether you are a:

Introvert (a reserved person, somebody focusing on his or her self)

(or)

Extrovert (an outgoing person)

It's about responding to God's promptings in your life. He knows better than you, what He's created you to do. When you hear God, feel God, have dreams, see yourself doing or saying things outside of your makeup, you'll begin to witness the supernatural hand of God at work through you ------- **stop** fighting and yield. You can't do anything if you don't move and you can't shake up anything if you don't speak up.

- **BE ABOUT IT, DON'T DOUBT IT!**

Proverbs 3:5-6, "Trust in the LORD with all thine heart; and lean not unto thine own understanding. In all thy ways acknowledge Him, and he shall direct thy paths."

Philippians 4:13, "I can do all things through Christ which strengtheneth me."

- **THERE'S NOTHING TO FEAR BUT FEAR IT-SELF**

II Timothy 1:7 "For God hath not given us the spirit of fear; but of power, and of love, and of a sound mind."

II Corinthians 10:4-5, "For the weapons of our warfare are not carnal, but mighty through God to the pulling down of strong holds. Casting down imaginations, and every high thing that exalteth itself against the knowledge of God, and bringing into captivity every thought to the obedience of Christ."

Casting down meaning reject, dismiss, denounce, to let go of.

NOTE:

- I HAVE WHAT GOD SAYS I HAVE – HIS POWER

- I AM WHO GOD SAYS I AM – A MOVER and A SHAKER

THEREFORE, I WILL:

C. **DENOUNCE DEFEAT and ANTICIPATE VICTORY!**

- Life is a challenge! It's as unpredictable as the weather; don't let the vicissitudes of life discombobulate you!

- Living and working for the Lord is a challenge; but don't let trial tribulation, and persecution, deflate you!

NOTE: Some of us love a challenge, the more difficult it seems the more ignited we are to conquer it. Sometimes we will come to an immovable brick wall (frozen); crushed by a landslide (overwhelmed), have the rug pulled out from under us (unexpected catastrophes), even with all our efforts. But when we get to the place of doing all we can do; and it appears that nothing is happening, that's the time we should submit (succumb) to the only "POWER" that is greater than we are and greater than any obstacle or enemy that's in our way!

Ephesians 3:20, "Now unto Him that is able to do exceeding abundantly above all that we ask or think, according to the power that worketh in us."

Would this "Power" that works in us give God such a great testament of praise if it was not true? The "**POWER**" that works in us: **Think it** - and God will enlarge the scope of your thinking. **Ask for it -** God is saying don't regard any limits/hindrances, etc.

GOD WILL OUT DO HIMSELF ON YOUR BEHALF WHEN YOU ACTIVATE THE INDWELLING "POWER" YOU POSSESS!

The Power of "The Blood" / "The Holy Spirit" / "The Word of God" / and "Prayer"

- If God be for me

- I am more than a conqueror

- Greater is He in me

- Look up and live, help is on the way

- There is nothing too hard for God; all things are possible with God

USE WHAT YOU HAVE and GET WHAT YOU WANT!

What do you want?

How bad do you want it?

Can God do it?

STUDY NOTES

GOD SPEAKS WE LISTEN

Study Notes

_____

_____

_____

_____

_____

_____

_____

_____

_____

_____

_____

_____

_____

_____

_____

_____

_____

_____

_____

_____

'God Speaks, We Listen: A hermeneutic journey through the scriptures for spiritual growth and effective application.'

GOD SPEAKS WE LISTEN

Study Notes

_____

_____

_____

_____

_____

_____

_____

_____

_____

_____

_____

_____

_____

_____

_____

_____

_____

_____

_____

'God Speaks, We Listen: A hermeneutic journey through the scriptures for spiritual growth and effective application.'

GOD SPEAKS
WE LISTEN

Study Notes

_____

_____

_____

_____

_____

_____

_____

_____

_____

_____

_____

_____

_____

_____

_____

_____

_____

_____

_____

'God Speaks, We Listen: A hermeneutic journey through the scriptures for spiritual growth and effective application.'

GOD SPEAKS WE LISTEN
Study Notes

_____

_____

_____

_____

_____

_____

_____

_____

_____

_____

_____

_____

_____

_____

_____

_____

_____

_____

'God Speaks, We Listen: A hermeneutic journey through the scriptures for spiritual growth and effective application.'

GOD SPEAKS WE LISTEN

Study Notes

_____

_____

_____

_____

_____

_____

_____

_____

_____

_____

_____

_____

_____

_____

_____

_____

_____

_____

_____

_____

'God Speaks, We Listen: A hermeneutic journey through the scriptures for spiritual growth and effective application.'

LESSON 6

TAKE THE LOAD OFF

L E S S O N   6

"TAKE THE LOAD OFF!"

SCRIPTURE: **I Peter 5: 7-10**

TITLE: **Take the Load Off!**

SUBJECT: Let God do what He does best as it pertains to our wellbeing as we allow Him to teach us how to **diminish** (to decrease seriously) the <u>affect</u> (to move or disturb emotionally or mentally) of worrying.

PROPOSITION: I purpose to show the hearer the tools required to ward off (prevent the occurrence of; prevent from happening) worrying and how to use them: thereby granting them the ability to meet lifes challenges head-on without getting wiped out.

OBJECTIVE: I want the hearer to experience peace of mind and enjoy the freedom of releasing the load of burdens that is not theirs to carry.

This message is for you; or for someone connected to you who, in some way, affects you; or for someone you know and those connected to them that affects them.

- Do you find you have been so absorbed in a situation that you don't recognize yourself?

- Do you find yourself losing who you are because you are so caught up in those that are connected to you; what they are dealing with or what they are going through?

STUDY NOTES

- What stays on your mind that causes you: unrest, to lose your appetite, your hair to fall out, lose weight and you are not on a diet, you gain weight and you're not conscious of how much food you are eating, you are snappy or more snappy than usual, you feel sick - go to the doctor - he exams you and find nothing wrong? Is there something that you can do to change things or is it beyond anything that you can do?

- Does it concern you, when you put forth every effort to be what God wants you to be and you take "HITS" for choosing to do the right thing; sometimes feeling like the odd ball in the midst of the majority?

- Let alone having to deal with the practical day to day things that causes you to be loaded down.

DON'T LOSE HEART! (DON'T BE DISCOURAGED)

NOTE: The extent to which we worry has a lot to do with the duration of time as it relates to your given situation:

- If things would happen sooner than later, we wouldn't worry.

- But in most instances things happen later than sooner and that word WORRY" begins to magnify. (to cause to seem greater)

"WORRY" - to torment oneself with or suffer from disturbing thoughts; to torment with cares, anxiety, and trouble.

The effect of worrying is just like HIV untreated; it develops into AIDS and you are open to other opportunistic diseases. (Your immune system has weaken to the point that it cannot fight off infections, which makes you susceptible to whatever wants to attack your body:) but there is hope;

- If one has the will to live and fight and they are willing to cooperate with their physician: the doctor can create a medical regiment that will counteract the attack on your immune system; over time your health will improve.

Why do I make this comparison? (Worrying to HIV)

- "WORRY" will stagnate you!

- "WORRY" will suck the life out of you, because it comes with all of its Opportunistic Relatives; (self-pity, frustration, depression, helplessness, and hopelessness) to attack your mind.

NOTE: You will notice over time or others connected to you will notice that:

- You're frozen without flexibility - functioning but emotionally you are not there.

- Laughing and smiling, being the life of the party, but you know it's a pretence to hide your deep seated sadness.

NOTE: What seems to be just a phase you're going through could be a sign of an emergency alert; if ignored, could place you in the danger zone.

NOTE: When you allow "Worry", and its Opportunistic Relatives (self-pity, frustration, depression, helplessness, hopelessness), to be the main thrust of your thought

STUDY NOTES

87

STUDY NOTES

process; it could lead you to secretly indulging in a self-relief method to ease your anxiety. If you are not careful; you will find yourself addicted to a habit that will become a greater challenge to break.

I Peter 5:7 KJV: Cast, etc. The Greek word for "cast" is ballo – which means to deposit with or to commit to. The Greek word for "cares" is merimma – which means anxiety, or a fearful painful uneasiness of mind: He Cares in the Greek, is melei – which means you are the object of His care.

I Peter 5:7 (TLB) says, "Let Him (God) have all your worries and cares, for he is always thinking about you and watching everything that concerns you."

NOTE: It is in our vulnerable places in life that the devil knit picks at our spirit, wanting to take residence in our minds; to break down our spiritual immune system.

I Peter 5:8 reads "Be sober, be vigilant; because your adversary the devil, as a roaring lion, walketh about, seeking whom he may devour."

Be careful - watch out for attacks from Satan, your great enemy, he prowls around like a hungry, roaring lion, looking for some victim to tear apart.

In my study of this text, it caused me to ask God 2 questions. How do I give God all my worries along with the Opportunistic Relatives that accompany it? How do I ward off (prevent the occurrence of or prevent from happening) the attacks of Satan?

LOOK AT THIS DICHOTOMY! (Division into two mutually opposed groups.)

- **GOD CARING TO GIVE YOU WELL FOUNDED CONFIDENGE**

- **SATAN ATTACKING TO TEAR YOU APART**

NOTE: There is one thing you must remember, you are the *Key* player in all of this. You determine how your situation will turn out based on what you know and how you utilize that knowledge. **Faith gives you knowledge and trust enables you to activate that knowledge.**

FAITH: "So then faith cometh by hearing, and hearing by the word of God." **Romans 10:17**

The Study of The Word of God: who "God" is; what "God" can do; how "God" feels about you; what "God" wants you to have; what "God" wants you to do/not do; exposes the prince of the air, "Satan", who hates "God" and all mankind. He's diligent at enticing the world to do evil and holds hostage the minds of those who are not aware that he is a defeated foe – he was defeated at CALVARY! It also lets you know that you have power and you're armed to win the battle.

Faith is bringing everything you know about God to the forefront (the position of greatest importance) and holding Him to it. Trust equips you with fortitude to persevere; assuring you you're not alone. Trust God - totally rely on God's ability to be who He is, allowing Him to do what he does.

The subject was not Take A load off (which implies there will be others you will carry), but TAKE THE LOAD OFF - finding a way to rid yourself of carrying any load at all.

STUDY NOTES

How do I give God all my worries along with the Opportunistic relatives that accompany it? We need to learn how to "cope" (to face and deal with responsibilities, problems or difficulties in a calm manner).

A. PUSH (PRAY UNTIL SOMETHING HAPPENS)

We are to avoid worrying and distracting thoughts in difficulties of life

- "WORRY" and "Opportunistic Relatives" disrupt your thoughts with a lot of noise and impairs your hearing.

- "WORRY" and "Opportunistic Relatives" can bring in the feeling of desperation and cause you to make irrational decisions.

- "WORRY" and "Opportunistic Relatives" will have you so self-absorbed, it will breakdown your ability to have "FAITH" in God and "Trust Him"

NOTE: "But without faith it is impossible to please him: for He that cometh to God must believe that he is, and that he is a rewarder of them that diligently seek him." **Hebrews 11:6.**

When you don't hold God to what He said; you are telling God that He is incapable of handling your situation and when you don't trust in Him, you are telling God, He is powerless!

NOTE: God wants to be all you need and do for you at all times but you have to free Him up and give Him free reign in your life!

Matt 6:25-32— "Therefore I say unto you, take no thought for your life, what ye shall eat, or what ye shall drink;

90

nor yet for your body, what ye shall put on. Is not the life more than meat, and the body than raiment? Behold the fowls of the air: for they sow not, neither do they reap, nor gather into barns; yet your heavenly Father feedeth them. Are ye not much better than they? Which of you by taking thought can add one cubit unto his stature? And why take ye thought for raiment? Consider the lilies of the field, how they grow; they toil not, neither do they spin: And yet I say unto you, That even Solomon in all his glory was not arrayed like one of these. Wherefore, if God so clothe the grass of the field, which to day is, and to morrow is cast into the oven, shall he not much more clothe you, O ye of little faith? Therefore take no thought, saying, What shall we eat? or, What shall we drink? or, Wherewithal shall we be clothed? (For after all these things do the Gentiles seek:) for your heavenly Father knoweth that ye have need of all these things."

Don't worry about what you're going to eat, drink, or wear; God knows you need these things.

Phil 4:6 (TLB) – "Don't worry about anything; instead, pray about everything; tell God your needs, and don't forget to thank him for his answers."

1Thess 5:17 – "Pray without ceasing."

Luke 18:1 – "And he spake a parable unto them to this end, that men ought always to pray, and not to faint."

E. M. Bounds -- The Complete Works on Prayer

E.M. Bounds writes, that prayer is the sovereign (capable of having the desired result and or effect) remedy, it's the antidote against perplexing worries and anxieties. **Prayer is a voice that goes into "God's" ear. God hears**

STUDY NOTES

the prayers of those who trust him and He's going to do something about what He hears!

NOTE: At those times in our lives when things are distorted, discombobulated, unravelled and we're loaded down from the cares of life -- WE NEED TO PRAY and cry out to the Lord

Help, Help, Lord I need your Help - asking for His support and direction.

Song: I Must Tell Jesus

I must tell Jesus all of my trials;

I cannot bear these burdens alone;

In my distress He kindly will help me;

He ever loves and cares for His own.

PRAYER brings the calm in the midst of the storm: **Phil 4:7** – "And the peace of God, which passeth all understanding, shall keep your hearts and minds through Christ Jesus."

Phil 4:8 -- Readjust your thoughts: "Finally, brethren, whatsoever things *are* true, whatsoever things *are* honest, whatsoever things *are* just, whatsoever things *are* pure, whatsoever things *are* lovely, whatsoever things *are* of good report; if *there b*e any virtue, and if *there be* any praise, think on these things."

If there be any virtue (conformity of one's life, conduct to moral and ethical principles), **praise**; **THINK ON THESE THINGS!!** "**PRAYER**" will keep you on alert and attentive to hear the Voice of God through whatever means he chooses to respond.

B. BE STEDFAST (UNWAVERING OR DETERMINED IN PURPOSE)

How do I ward-off (prevent the occurrence of or prevent from happening) the attacks of Satan? Your resolve in life should be, "I Shall Live and not Die!" When you make that declaration you know something!

1. You must know who you are up against; he wants to destroy you; **I Peter 5:8** says **"Satan is like a roaring lion seeking to tear you apart"** – he is the father of all lies, deceiver, accuser of the brethren, the evil one, murderer, ruler of the powers of darkness, prince of power of the air, tempter, thief, destroyer defeated foe at Calvary;

2. You know you have the Power to fight; you're equipped to win the battle. **Ephesians 6:10** – "Finally, my brethren, be strong in the Lord, and in the power of his might."

Ephesians 6:11 – "Put on the whole armour of God, that ye may be able to stand against the wiles of the devil." **(lion/gird yourself with truth** - no deceit/hypocrisy); **(breastplate of righteousness**-integrity); **(feet shod with the preparation of gospel of peace** - a doer of the word); **(shield of faith** - stop arrows aim by/Satan); **(helmet of salvation** –deliver you from the power of sin); **(sword of the spirit – the Word of God** -living actively the Word – sharper than 2-edge sword – discerner of the thoughts and intents of the heart). Pray always.

3. You know who is in your corner; who supports you - THE SOVEREIGN GOD, Power of the Holy Spirit. Verses 9 and 10 says: Stand Firm and Trust God - as you weather the onslaughts of life God will restore you; give you some back bone and make you strong.

STUDY NOTES

NOTE: If one is to "Be Steadfast", you must get rid of the things that will cause you to waver (alternation between one direction or another).

God is not going to abracadabra our situation away. "Iron sharpens Iron." Sometimes we need counselling. Have someone in your life you can trust to talk to. Talk to a professional be verbal or you will implode.

When you pray and ask him for guidance, He will provide a means to bring the right people that can assist you. He can open the avenue whereby you will gain access to help, insight and/or a resolution.

If God be for you, who can be against you. When the load is lifted, you can breathe again, and see life through new eyes. Submit yourself to the service and work of God knowing full well that He rescued you; then God will be able to use you to help others find their way.

SONGS

<u>Reach Out and Touch Somebody's Hand</u>

Reach out and touch
Somebody's hand
Make this world a better place
If you can
Reach out and touch
Somebody's hand
Make this world a better place
If you can

<u>What the World Needs Now is Love</u>

What the world needs now is love sweet love,
It's the only thing that there's just too little of.

What the world needs now is love sweet love,
No not just for some but for everyone.

He Ain't Heavy, He's My Brother

The road is long
With many a winding turn
That leads us to who knows where
Who knows when
But I'm strong
Strong enough to carry him
He ain't heavy, he's my brother

God Is

God is the joy and the strength of my life
Removes all pain, misery and strife
He promised to keep me never leave me
He'll never, never fall short of His Word
I've got to fast and pray, stay in the narrow way
I'll keep my life clean everyday.
I want to go with Him when He comes back.
I've come too far and I'll never turn back.
God is, God is, God is, God is. God is my all and all.

GOD SPEAKS WE LISTEN

Study Notes

_____

_____

_____

_____

_____

_____

_____

_____

_____

_____

_____

_____

_____

_____

_____

_____

_____

_____

'God Speaks, We Listen: A hermeneutic journey through the scriptures for spiritual growth and effective application.'

GOD SPEAKS WE LISTEN

Study Notes

_____

_____

_____

_____

_____

_____

_____

_____

_____

_____

_____

_____

_____

_____

_____

_____

_____

_____

_____

_____

'God Speaks, We Listen: A hermeneutic journey through the scriptures for spiritual growth and effective application.'

GOD SPEAKS WE LISTEN

Study Notes

_____
_____
_____
_____
_____
_____
_____
_____
_____
_____
_____
_____
_____
_____
_____
_____
_____
_____
_____

'God Speaks, We Listen: A hermeneutic journey through the scriptures for spiritual growth and effective application.'

GOD SPEAKS WE LISTEN

Study Notes

_____

_____

_____

_____

_____

_____

_____

_____

_____

_____

_____

_____

_____

_____

_____

_____

_____

_____

'God Speaks, We Listen: A hermeneutic journey through the scriptures for spiritual growth and effective application.'

GOD SPEAKS WE LISTEN

Study Notes

_____

_____

_____

_____

_____

_____

_____

_____

_____

_____

_____

_____

_____

_____

_____

_____

_____

_____

_____

'God Speaks, We Listen: A hermeneutic journey through the scriptures for spiritual growth and effective application.'

LESSON 7

THE POWER OF WORDS

LESSON 7

"THE POWER OF WORDS!"

SCRIPTURE: **I Chronicles 29:11-12 / II Corinthians 13:5 / Lamentations 3:40 / I Corinthians 9:27 / I Corinthians 10:12 / Ephesians 4:14 / Ephesians 5:15-16 / I Corinthians 15:58**

TITLE: **The Power of Words!**

SUBJECT: **The Power of Words!**

PROPOSITION: I purpose to show the hearer the importance of choosing and using words that will empower them to maintain so they can be sustained through this journey of life.

OBJECTIVE: I want the hearer to know that they will have the power to confront any issue in life they will encounter with a victorious mind-set.

Today I want to remind you of a few things, spark your interest, and indelibly inscribe in your mind some selective words that will enable you to cope with life: be it spiritual, natural, or practical.

REMIND YOU THAT:

God is the creator and we are the creation, molded and fashioned in God's image. We are the benefactors of his precious gift of life and endowed with "the essence of Himself" within us. We are born into this world as "Spiritual Beings", housed in a human body. We are spiritu-

STUDY NOTES

al beings on a human journey: not a human being on a spiritual journey. We are not born as "Human Being" in search of that spiritual connection. Our lives are God-centered from the beginning and it should be God centered throughout our tenure here on earth: to ultimately fulfill the purpose of God for our lives.

"PICTURE THIS"

You were born a vessel of honor, to become a visual figure of God in the earth; so, you can be the salt and light that will influence and impact the world individually and collectively. You will show the world, there is an Ultimate ruler that wants to make the best out of everything mankind encounters: to lift them up and they in turn will always glorify God. (PERFECT CONCEPT). God didn't have all these ideals of us and set us up to fail. He knew man would fall so he set in motion his masterful plan of Reconciliation.

Jesus Christ - Propitiation - (complete satisfaction for God's wrath against sin)

Jesus Christ – Redeemer – (paid the price for you and me; the righteousness of God)

Ephesians 2:8-9, "For by grace are we saved through faith; and that not of ourselves: It is a gift of God: Not of works, lest any man should boast."

LIVE LONG ENOUGH -- LIFE HAS A WAY OF TAINTING and SCARRING YOU! FULL OF ROAD BLOCKS, CROSSROADS, PITFALLS, SETBACKS, DISTRACTIONS, AND TEMPTATIONS.

4 Questions:

1. How can we be all God wants us to be?

2. How do we do all God wants us to do?

3. How do we handle the spiritual, natural and practical things of life?

4. How can we stay on course?

Well, you need to be smart. **Matthew 10:16b** – "…be ye therefore wise as serpents, and harmless as doves." To be wise, one must have "Wisdom" (to act utilizing knowledge, experience, understanding, common sense, and insight)

THE POWER OF WORDS!

QUOTES: Jodi Picoult – "Words are like eggs dropped from great heights, you can no more call them back than ignore the mess they leave when they fall."

Paulo Coelho – "Of all the weapons of destruction that man could invent, the most terrible and the most powerful was the word. Daggers and spears left traces of blood, arrows could be seen at a distance. Poisons were detected in the end and avoided. But the word managed to destroy without leaving clues."

Patrick Rothfuss – "Words can light fires in the minds of men; words can ring tears from the hardest heart."

What does "POWER" mean – the ability to do or act; accomplishing something; strength (mental power-of or pertaining to the mind) (moral power-capable of conforming to the rules of right conduct); to give power to; make powerful.

What gives a "WORD" power? Knowing its definition and making it applicable to a given circumstance or situation. **WORDS can DEVOUR, INTIMIDATE, DEVESTATE, TEAR YOU DOWN, ARE HARSH, KIND, BUILD YOU UP, EDUCATE, MOTIVATE, INSPIRE, AND EMPOWER.**

5 WORDS

I have "5" words I want to earmark that will empower you to cope with life: be it spiritual, natural, or practical.

1. **SOVEREIGNTY** (supreme and unrestricted power; Dominion of God, His absolute right to do all things according to His own good pleasure) **I Chronicles 29:11-12 (NKJV)**, "Yours Oh Lord, is the greatness. The power and the glory. The victory and the majesty; of all that is in heaven and in the earth is Yours; Yours is the kingdom, O Lord, and you are exalted as Head over all. Both riches and honor come from you, and You reign over all. In your hand is Power and Might; in your hand it is to make great and to give strength to all."

   • God is the creator, orchestrator, regulator, demonstrator, and emancipator.

   Acts 17:28 (NKJV) – "For in him we live, and move, and have our being; as certain also of your own poets have said, for we are also His offspring."

   • Who you are -- God made you.

- What you have -- God gave you.

- What you know -- God taught you.

- Where you are -- God brought you.

2. **SELF-EXAMINATION** - (scrutinize thoroughly; to examine in detail w/careful attention)

II Corinthians 13:5a "Examine yourselves, whether ye be in the faith; prove your own selves."

Lamentations 3:40, "Let us search and try our ways and turn again to the Lord."

I Corinthians 9:27 Paul states, "But I keep under my body, and bring it into subjection: lest that by any means, when I have preached to others, I myself should be a castaway."

- Have self-control

- Restrain those sinful appetites

- Self-denial

- Mortify the flesh

NOTE: Remember you are serving a SOVEREIGN God who will not come down to our standards but you must rise up to His standards.

3. **CONSISTENCY** – (adherence to the same principles, course)

I Corinthians 10:12 – "Wherefore let him that thinketh he standeth take heed lest he fall."

STUDY NOTES

St. John 15:1-5 – "I am the true vine, and my Father is the husbandman. Every branch in me that beareth not fruit he taketh away: and every branch that beareth fruit, he purgeth it, that it may bring forth more fruit. Now ye are clean through the word which I have spoken unto you. Abide in me, and I in you. As the branch cannot bear fruit of itself, except it abide in the vine; no more can ye, except ye abide in me. I am the vine, ye are the branches: He that abideth in me, and I in him, the same bringeth forth much fruit: for without me ye can do nothing."

Ephesians 4:14 – "That we henceforth be no more children (gullible, vulnerable, easily victimized), tossed to and fro, and carried about with every wind of doctrine, by the sleight of men, and cunning craftiness, whereby they lie in wait to deceive"

Speak the truth in love (all that believers say and do should be honest and true and said or done in a loving manner), **and grow up** (stability and integrity) **in all things edifying Jesus Christ**

- Keep your eye on the Prize, know your place and stay in place; know where you fit in the scheme of God's plan - Disciple (student, learner, pupil, follower/JC, apprentice) carrying out the Great Commission (Go and make Disciples in all nations, baptizing in name the Father, the Son and the Holy Ghost and teach them to obey the commands I give you).

NOTE: Your relationship with God is not confined to a Sunday worship or bible study experience; it is a day to day interaction. Being a doer of the word even when it conflicts against your will. You don't live for God based on your terms but His.

NOTE: When it comes to being Consistent: What can I do differently than I've been doing or doing now? It's not so much about doing it differently, it's about being <u>consistent</u>! (adherence to the same principles, course)

    a.   Stay Humble - (freedom from arrogance) Humble yourself under the mighty hand of God. Keep your ego in check, make sure your motives are pure, don't be a wolf in sheep's clothing.

    b.   Stay Focused - **Ephesians 6:12** – "For we wrestle not against flesh and blood, but against principalities, against powers, against the rulers of the darkness of this world, against spiritual wickedness in high places."

II Corinthians 10:4-6 – "For the weapons of our warfare are not carnal, but mighty through God to the pulling down of strong holds; Casting down imaginations, and every high thing that exalteth itself against the knowledge of God, and bringing into captivity every thought to the obedience of Christ; and having in a readiness to revenge all disobedience, when your obedience is fulfilled."

    c.   Stay Prayerful - Prayer is a shield to the soul, a sacrifice to God and an infliction of punishment for Satan. (John Bunyan)

    d.   Men ought always pray, etc. Pray without ceasing. Prayer is not a monologue, but a dialogue (talking to God; it's thinking about God; communication with God; it's speaking to God; and waiting until God speaks back).

e. **Jas 5:16b** "The effectual (expected result), fervent (intensity of spirit) prayer of a righteous man avails much."

f. <u>The Power of Prayer is not the result of the person praying: rather the power resides in the God who is being prayed to!</u>

4. **DETERMINATION** – (to come to a decision or resolution)

I Corinthians 15:58 – "Therefore, my beloved brethren, be ye steadfast, unmoveable, always abounding in the work of the Lord, forasmuch as ye know that your labour is not in vain in the Lord."

a. Be steadfast, unmovable, always abounding (keep working) in the work/Lord, etc.

b. Be Faithful – (**dependable, loyal, stable, as it pertains to your relationship w/God and that of your fellowman**)

c. Be Inseparable – (incapable of being separated; parted; disjoined) – "For I am persuaded, that neither death, nor life, nor angels, nor principalities, nor powers, nor things present, nor things to come, Nor height, nor depth, nor any other creature, shall be able to separate us from the love of God, which is in Christ Jesus our Lord."

5. **PERCEPTION** - (to recognize, discern, envision, or understand; come to comprehend; grasp) Proverbs 4:7 – "Wisdom is the principal thing; therefore get wisdom: and with all thy getting get understanding."

NOTE: Ones perception is relative to their knowledge about a given subject/issue; and with knowledge we must have a clear understanding. Knowledge (information) without clarity can result in a misconception. Your perception right or wrong influences everything else you do. THAT'S LIFE ON EVERY LEVEL!

- <u>Your perception needs to be "Sharp"; not a know it all; but "Alert" Keen".</u>

    a. keeping a watchful eye to ward off deception

    b. Listening intently so you can hear pass what you heard

- This Christian journey is not about nonsense, or profit: it's about an aggressive, progressive, strategic, movement of overcoming, losing a few battles but winning the war. That you may be solidified and GOD being glorified.

Ephesians 5:15-16 – "See then that ye walk circumspectly, not as fools, but as wise, Redeeming the time, because the days are evil."

II Timothy 3:1 – "This know also, that in the last days perilous times shall come."

Matthew 11:12 – "And from the days of John the Baptist until now the kingdom of heaven suffereth violence, and the violent take it by force."

John 10:10, "The thief (Satan) cometh not, but for to steal, and to kill, and to destroy: I (Jesus Christ) am come that they might have life, and that they might have it more abundantly.

Satan:

- Comes to steal your joy

- Kill your influence

- Destroy your character

- Make you fail. Your failures are not for you to give up but an opportunity for you to rise up.

Jesus:

- Jesus Christ said, "I am come that you have life"

- "Many are the afflictions of the righteous: but the LORD delivereth him out of them all." **Psalms 34:19**

- "I have been young, and now am old; yet have I not seen the righteous forsaken, nor his seed begging bread." **Psalm 37:25**

- "But they that wait upon the LORD shall renew their strength; they shall mount up with wings as eagles; they shall run, and not be weary; and they shall walk, and not faint." **Isaiah 40:31**

- "Come unto me, all ye that labor and are heavy laden, and I will give you rest. Take my yoke upon you, and learn of me; for I am meek and lowly in heart: and ye shall find rest unto your souls." **Matthew 11:28-29**

Why do you exist? **The Sovereignty of God.**

What will keep you fit for the Masters use? **Self-Examination**

How do you remain stable? **<u>Consistency</u>**.

How do you handle distraction? **<u>Determination</u>**.

What will keep you in ready alert? **<u>Perception</u>**.

GOD SPEAKS WE LISTEN

Study Notes

‐‐

'God Speaks, We Listen: A hermeneutic journey through the scriptures for spiritual growth and effective application.'

GOD SPEAKS WE LISTEN
Study Notes

_____

_____

_____

_____

_____

_____

_____

_____

_____

_____

_____

_____

_____

_____

_____

_____

_____

_____

_____

'God Speaks, We Listen: A hermeneutic journey through the scriptures for spiritual growth and effective application.'

GOD SPEAKS WE LISTEN

Study Notes

_____
_____
_____
_____
_____
_____
_____
_____
_____
_____
_____
_____
_____
_____
_____
_____
_____
_____
_____

'God Speaks, We Listen: A hermeneutic journey through the scriptures for spiritual growth and effective application.'

GOD SPEAKS WE LISTEN
Study Notes

_____
_____
_____
_____
_____
_____
_____
_____
_____
_____
_____
_____
_____
_____
_____
_____
_____
_____
_____
_____
_____

'God Speaks, We Listen: A hermeneutic journey through the scriptures for spiritual growth and effective application.'

GOD SPEAKS
WE LISTEN

Study Notes

_____

_____

_____

_____

_____

_____

_____

_____

_____

_____

_____

_____

_____

_____

_____

_____

_____

_____

'God Speaks, We Listen: A hermeneutic journey through the scriptures for spiritual growth and effective application.'

LESSON 8

PRAYER STILL WORKS

LESSON 8

"PRAYER STILL WORKS!"

SCRIPTURE: **II Chronicles 7:14 and James 5:16b**

TITLE: **Prayer Still Works!**

SUBJECT: **Prayer Still Works!**

PROPOSITION: I purpose to show the hearer that living an upright life before God is a staple which guarantees that God will answer your prayer.

OBJECTIVE: I want the hearer to be cognizant of the magnitude of the scope prayer as it pertains to the world, mankind, and one's self.

Let's delve into something you already know. Encourage you to use that knowledge to your advantage: because "Knowledge is Power"! The "Power" obtained based on what you know will enable you to "Defuse" the effect of uncertainty and be "Infused" with certainty.

- it's an affirmative that alleviates a query.

- it's a positive that overrules a negative.

- it's an assurance that does not vacillate.

- it solidifies a bond that can't be severed.

PRAYER STILL WORKS!!!!!!!!!!!!!

NOTE: GOD AWAITS YOUR EARNEST REQUEST SO HE CAN RESPOND WITH A UNDENIABLE IMPACT!!

STUDY NOTES

QUESTION?? Can we approach God in any kind of condition? NO!!

NOTE: If you notice the text refers to a <u>R</u>ighteous <u>M</u>an (<u>person</u>). What denotes a "R" "P"?

**Righteous - conformance to established standards of morality, justice, or uprightness. "R" "P" - one who is following the ways of God!!!!!

NOTE:

So, if we are to approach God on his terms, there are some things we must do:

**II Chronicles 7:14, "If my people, which are called by my name, shall humble themselves, and pray, and seek my face, and turn from their wicked ways; then will I hear from heaven, and will forgive their sin, and will heal their land."

"If my people which are called by my name, shall…"

1. **HUMBLE** – themselves - recognize your frailties without God's help.

2. **PRAY** – prayer and helplessness are inseparable. Only those who are helpless can truly pray…. "Your helplessness is your best prayer" **<u>PRAYER OPENS THE CHANNEL FOR GOD TO DEAL WITH YOU</u>**".

3. **SEEK MY FACE** –when you seek God's face, it's not about what you want from God or need him to do; it's about what God wants from you and what God needs you to do: in other words

4. **TURN FROM THEIR WICKED WAYS** – repent with contrition - a renewed adaptation. Getting things in order that are out of order. Get aligned with God's methods.

5. **THEN I WILL HEAR FROM HEAVEN** – you will have God's attention and he will implement a plan.

6. **FORGIVE THEIR SIN** -- those things that God doesn't want us to do, be, have, or engage in that will draw us further away from him.

7. **HEAL THEIR LAND** -- Our disconnect from God has caused brokenness and open wounds. God wants more for us then we want for ourselves. When God heals their land, expect a "Paradigm Shift". That's when you **move** from **one model of thinking** to a **completely different way of thinking** – God will reverse his judgment for your sin(s) and restore you.

    a. Instead of disobedience there will be obedience

    b. That which is barren becomes fertile

    c. What has been destroyed is restored

    d. That which is incomplete is made whole

James 5:16b (KJV) The Effectual Fervent Prayer of a Righteous Man Availeth Much!!!!

James 5:16b (NLT) The Earnest Prayer of a Righteous Person has Great Power and Productive Results!!!!!

James 5:16b (Message) The Prayer of a person Living right with God is something Powerful to be Reckoned with.

STUDY NOTES

James 5:16b (Voice Bible) Your Prayers are Powerful when they are rooted in a righteous life.

- **EFFECTUAL** – something positive and fruitfully happens.

- **FERVENT** – intensity of spirit; feeling enthusiasm

- **PRAYER** – Is not a monologue but a dialogue -- talking with God; it is thinking about God; communication with God. It's speaking to God and waiting until God speaks back. PRAYER is a shield to the soul; a sacrifice to God; and an infliction of punishment for Satan.... **John Bunyan**

- **Of A RIGHTEOUS MAN** – conformance to established standards – refers to following the ways of God.

- **AVAILETH MUCH** – a goal is achieved/accomplished.

I Peter 3:12a, the eyes of the Lord are over the righteous, and his ears are open unto their prayers

**PRAYER STILL WORKS

NOTE: **When we approach God on his terms and submit to God's instructions, he will grant our petition.**

* Therefore, we must stay aligned with God.

I Peter 4:7b - Be serious and watchful in your prayers!!!

3 main points of emphasis – FOCUSED, STEADY & READY!!!

A. FOCUSED (TO CONCENTRATE; TO FOCUS ONE'S THOUGHTS)

Luke 18:1 – Jesus told his disciples to always pray and not give up!!

- Loves God with all their heart, soul, strength & above all else.

- Have a relationship with God; Jesus Christ – Savior; filled with Holy Ghost.

- Not just a hearer of the Word but a doer of the Word.

- You're not one who just quotes scripture, but diligently studies the Word of God. Dissects it to obtain clarity; have understanding which enables you to walk in wisdom, live a life of obedience with integrity.

- You know yourself - self examination, works on your flaws, knows you need counsel: accepts correction.

- Can handle criticism: they will eat the meat and discard the bones.

- Will have a person in your life that will remind you that your stuff stinks.

- You will forgive when you have been rejected, misused, lied on or offended.

STUDY NOTES

- Don't regress to a pity pot, wallow in depression or lose it when things don't go their way.

- Choose their battles: you know the ones you need to fight and know the ones that only God can fight for you.

- You are watchful (interactive yet observing their surroundings)

- See with an extra eye - discernment.

- Listen to gossip: I don't mean you listen on purpose, the gossiper will find you and you will crack their face by stating – let's go to God in prayer right now on their behalf.

- You do not go along to get along.

- Seek God for direction before they make a move.

B. STEADY (STEADFAST, OR UNWAVERING, RESOLUTE, A STEADY PURPOSE)

NOTE: **THE "POWER OF PRAYER" IS NOT THE RESULT OF THE PERSON PRAYING; RATHER, THE "POWER" RESIDES IN THE GOD WHO IS BEING PRAYED TO.**

- You are not so heavenly bound that you are no earthly good.

- You do not live in your own world -- but you are up to date about what's happening in the world you live in:

a. **Spiritually** -- we are disciples emulating the Master Teacher; we are witnesses of God's saving grace & awesome Power.

b. **Economics** -- the haves will not discard the have nots/poor; nor take advantage of those that have some/ middle class.

c. **Politics** -- representatives will stop using their constituents when they need a vote & bamboozle them once they are in office. Leaders with integrity, there will be justice for all men, concern for all, and willing to stand up & fight for what's right.

d. **Military** -- Co-man/Chief, House/Sen, will be wise in judgment in deploying soldiers, securing the nation, & treat our veterans with honor.

e. **Education** -- from pre-school to college level; stop cutting school budgets, cancelling school grants, every person deserves a qualified education.

f. **Health** -- (Physical/Mental) -- every person can obtain affordable "HC" & not reverse what's good for the whole to appease a few.

g. **Prison System**- reverse laws that prohibit return citizens from succeeding and using the "P-S" as a get rich entity for the greedy.

h. **Social media** - a good thing/used for good (it will get you exposure but what you put out there will stay out there; it's never deleted and in some instances, it's a cesspool of evil.

k. **Entertainment**- a good thing but some of it has subliminal & blatant messages that corrupt, and all PG13 in not PG13.

STUDY NOTES

1. **The Human Race**-state and fate of mankind of all ages ("OS / "NS")

Old School - anything that if from an earlier era or anything that can be considered "old fashioned".

New School - anything contemporary. "NS" is about being agents of change in society which is hip, with it, in fashion.

"DIFFERENCE DOES NOT MEAN DIVISION!!!"

NOTE:

Being "OS" does not give you cart blanch to be condescending toward those you consider "NS".

Being "NS" does not give you cart blanch to be condescending toward those you consider "OS".

"OS" - your longevity in life experiences may have afforded you some wisdom but you don't know everything.

"NS" - your inexperience does not disqualify you from being viable.

"THE "OS" & "NS" NEED EACH OTHER", until we begin to understand this, there will only be the brooding of the divide and no coming together.

***Don't make judgment calls, you don't know folks story. As we speak; someone is going through hard times, about to give up, heartbroken, stressed, worried about how they are going to make ends meet, overwhelmed about family matters; dealing with trauma, frustrated due to rejection.

C. READY (Completely prepared or in fit condition for immediate action or use)

NOTE: A righteous person who prays takes on many identities: you are a worshipper, supplicant, petitioner, intercessor, and warrior.

**Ephesians 6:18 (Weymouth "NT") - Pray with unceasing prayer and entreaty on every fitting occasion in the spirit, and be always on the alert to seize opportunities for doing so: with unwearied persistence and entreaty on behalf of all God's people.

REMEMBER: The Word of God (Bible) is the arsenal that will supply every Spiritually Mature and Empowered believer to fight the good fight of faith because there is work to do:

- Represent the Kingdom of God on earth.

- Be fortified in your Faith.

- You are God's mouthpiece. He has enabled you to exult, reprove, and rebuke those that need direction; you are like seasoning:

   1. a delicate hint -- enrich their palate -- encourage them

   2. a touch of heat -- get their attention -- a slap on the wrist

   3. Extreme heat - no compromise or bias opinion - you declare God's truth to them.

- Be gladiators in destroying the satanic influence upon mankind:

STUDY NOTES

a. Recognize the devil when you see him.

b. Put the devil in his place.

c. Be ready to take him down. He is a defeated foe!

d. Cast down all strongholds and every imagination that exults itself above God.

e. Bridge the gap for the feeble *(weak intellectually or morally; lacking force, strength, or effectiveness)* and uphold *(to maintain, affirm, or defend against opposition of challenge)*, the strong *(of great moral power, firmness or courage)!!!!!*

f. **AN ADEQUATE PRAYER LIFE ERUPTS WITH RADICAL PRAISE!!!!!!!!!!!**

GOD SPEAKS WE LISTEN

Study Notes

_____

_____

_____

_____

_____

_____

_____

_____

_____

_____

_____

_____

_____

_____

_____

_____

_____

_____

'God Speaks, We Listen: A hermeneutic journey through the scriptures for spiritual growth and effective application.'

GOD SPEAKS WE LISTEN

Study Notes

_____

_____

_____

_____

_____

_____

_____

_____

_____

_____

_____

_____

_____

_____

_____

_____

_____

_____

_____

'God Speaks, We Listen: A hermeneutic journey through the scriptures for spiritual growth and effective application.'

GOD SPEAKS WE LISTEN

Study Notes

_____

_____

_____

_____

_____

_____

_____

_____

_____

_____

_____

_____

_____

_____

_____

_____

_____

_____

_____

_____

'God Speaks, We Listen: A hermeneutic journey through the scriptures for spiritual growth and effective application.'

GOD SPEAKS WE LISTEN

Study Notes

_____

_____

_____

_____

_____

_____

_____

_____

_____

_____

_____

_____

_____

_____

_____

_____

_____

_____

'God Speaks, We Listen: A hermeneutic journey through the scriptures for spiritual growth and effective application.'

GOD SPEAKS WE LISTEN

Study Notes

_____

_____

_____

_____

_____

_____

_____

_____

_____

_____

_____

_____

_____

_____

_____

_____

_____

_____

'God Speaks, We Listen: A hermeneutic journey through the scriptures for spiritual growth and effective application.'

LESSON 9

LOVE'S IN NEED OF LOVE TODAY

LESSON 9

"LOVE'S IN NEED OF LOVE TODAY!"

SCRIPTURE: **St. John 13:34-35**

TITLE: **Love's in Need of Love Today!**

SUBJECT: **Show Your Love**

PROPOSITION: I purpose to show the hearer that Jesus wants love to be the guiding principal in how we interact with one another which makes us identifiable with his inclination in loving.

OBJECTIVE: I want the hearer to start seeing love through God's eyes by expressing love toward their fellowman with no holds barred.

Have you ever gone to church and Praise and Worship was good; choir good, then it's time for the message; scripture read, subject announced and you say ah, this one is not for me and you zone out? Sitting there twitching, you want to leave while the preacher is preaching but that would be disrespectful, so you get your cell phone and start texting/tweeting or you do a replay in your mind about how good or bad your week was or thinking about what you are going to do when you leave church?

What I like about coming into the physical building called church, it's made clear to me that I am more than a human being; I'm a spiritual being too. When the human part of

STUDY NOTES

me zones out, the spiritual part of me is always zoned in to the voice of God.

God knows what you need to hear when you don't want to hear it.

God knows what you should do but you are resistant in doing it.

God knows what you need to do to change your circumstance and you are dead set on not changing.

God knows you better than you know yourself: He can infiltrate your psyche better than anyone or anything else.

"LOVE'S IN NEED OF LOVE TODAY!"

Love can be oo~ee goo~ee - the vibes are right; the commonalties are balanced; the other person's happiness matters to you; you do everything to enhance that.

Then the love you had for someone can turn you into a monster when the scenario changes:

If you're heartbroken this is the last thing you want to hear.

If there is unforgiveness in your heart, a wall of resistance is up.

If you think you're right and everyone else is wrong; there is nothing anyone can say to you.

If you are loved starved, you ask where can I find it with pure intentions?

If you have a love deficient, you say I have given my all, I'm not appreciated.

PURPOSE: TO ENCOURAGE YOU TO START SEEING LOVE THROUGH GOD'S EYES AND NOT YOUR OWN!

Who is your biggest enemy? Yourself. And when it comes to dealing with self, a lot of self-deception is going on. There is some good, bad and ugly in all of us.

If you are going to love someone, you can't just love part of the package (baggage); but must love all of the package, (baggage).

Your Good is an encouragement that you respond to a higher power than yourself, which enables you to decipher right and wrong, moral and immoral; justice and injustice; selfless and selfishness.

Your Bad breaks the natural law-Jail – **your Bad** breaks the spiritual law- deliverance

Your Ugly speaks against natural norms (insanity) – **your Ugly** speaks against the Spiritual norms – Repent

NOTE: When it comes to dealing with this tri-fold facet of our character (The Good, the Bad and the Ugly)

- We see the faults of others and we judge negatively

- we ignore our character defects and blame others

- we see the faults in ourselves and feel we can't rise above them so we begin to self-destruct

- we become blindsided, can't see pass what we see- there is a road block which hinders us from moving forward

God sees the fault but he looks beyond the fault and sees the need for salvation, sanctification, restoration,

STUDY NOTES

liberation and total victory.

SONG: Please Be Patient with Me

Please be patient with me,

God is not through with me yet.

Please be patient with me,

God is not through with me yet.

When God gets through with me,

when God gets through with me,

I shall come forth,

I shall come forth like pure gold.

Refined gold is soft and pliable; free from corrosion and other substances[ii]

- When it's mixed with other metals (copper, iron, nickel, and so on) it becomes hard, less pliable and more corrosive.

- The mixture is called an "alloy", the higher the % of foreign metals, the gold becomes harder: the lower the percent of alloy the softer and more flexible the gold becomes.

1. 1st step in refining gold is grinding it into a powder and mixing it with a substance called "FLUX".

2. Then the mixture is placed in a furnace and melted by intense heat.

---

ii   John Bevere – "The Bait of Satan" 1994 by Charisma House Book Group

3. The alloys and impurities are drawn to the "FLUX" and rise to the surface.

4. The Gold (which is heavier) remains at the bottom.

5. The impurities, (copper, iron, zinc, etc.) is then removed yielding a purer gold.

NOTE: Isaiah 48:10 – "Behold, I have refined thee, but not with silver; l have chosen thee in the furnace of affliction."

Malachi 3:2-3 – "But who may abide the day of his coming? and who shall stand when he appeareth? for he is like a refiner's fire, and like fullers' soap: And he shall sit as a refiner and purifier of silver: and he shall purify the sons of Levi, and purge them as gold and silver, that they may offer unto the LORD an offering in righteousness."

NOTE: So, if we are going to come forth as pure Gold, we must experience the intense heat of the fire (God refines us with trials, affliction and tribulation) which brings to the surface our impurities (sins/issues).

When we are in the refiner's fire, our resistance is broken and our ignorance is enlightened.

We become soft and pliable, open to hear God's voice clearly, repent of our sins, deal with our issues correctly, and be more considerate in our relating to others.

EXEGESIS: And so, I'm giving you a new commandment: love each other as much as I've loved you; your strong love for each other will prove to the world that you are my disciples.

STUDY NOTES

- This "**Commandment**" Jesus Christ said love one another. It's not an emotional love; it is the disciplined will to seek the welfare of others. This love is to be manifested in deeds!

- A "**Disciple**" is one who embraces and assists in spreading the teachings of another and imitates their practices.

Therefore I'm "OPEN" to the clarion call – Love's in need of love today!

I am a "RESPONDER" to God's need for love to be shown in the world!

I am the "INSTRUMENT" for the flow through of God's love!

Because I am a "RECIPIENT" of God's love!

NOTE: Ephesians 3:16-18, "That he would grant you, according to the riches of his glory, to be strengthened with might by his Spirit in the inner man; That Christ may dwell in your hearts by faith; that ye, being rooted and grounded in love, May be able to comprehend with all saints what is the breadth, and length, and depth, and height;"

A. GIVE LOVE

You know the fault(s) but see the need and you respond by fulfilling the need (**John 3:16**, "For God so loved the world, that he gave his only begotten Son, that whosoever believeth in him should not perish, but have everlasting life.")

- Not self-serving but self-sacrifice

- You show your true heart – genuine/no hidden agenda

- Speak to what is major – what matters most

- Give love, you look for change – love covers a multitude of sins

B. SHOW LOVE

Galatians 6:1 – "Brothers and sisters, if someone is caught in a sin, you who live by the Spirit should restore that person gently. But watch yourselves, or you also may be tempted."

NOTE: If one is going to "Show Love"; you must be Spiritual. What does it mean to be "Spiritual"?

- Your mind reflects the mind of God

- You move from Human reasoning to Divine reasoning

- You embrace the Truth of God with keen insight

- Your will is harmonized with the will of God

NOTE: Don't be like the Devil – **John 10:10a**, "The thief cometh not, but for to steal, and to kill, and to destroy:"

- Don't steal someone else's joy

- Kill their influence

- Destroy their character

- Don't hate/appreciate

- Don't judge/ restore

- Don't make mockery – lift up

- Don't gossip about people – talk to them directly

- Don't do bad to people like they have done bad to you – do good by them

- If you don't have anything good to say, don't say anything at all

- Husbands, your wife is not your daughter – don't talk to her any kind of way or when you feel like it (then you want her to be your woman later).

- Wives your husband is not your little boy – don't talk to him any kind of way or when you feel like it (then you want him to be your man later).

NOTE: Be like Jesus – John 10:10b, "I am come that they might have life, and that they might have it more abundantly."

- When you "show love", it brings out your best

- You take the right approach

- You are pro-active instead of reactive

- You're not emotional but purposeful

C. BE LOVING

Flow in Love like God does, you will feel better about yourself; this will make it easier as you relate to others.

NOTE: Loving others is a challenge. It's easy to love them if you don't deal with them; keep your distance. But you know you have the victory when you are interacting with them in spite of how they behave.

How do we become the loving people that God wants us to be?

Colossians 3:12, "Put on therefore, as the elect of God, holy and beloved, bowels of mercies, kindness, humbleness of mind, meekness, longsuffering"

Longsuffering- Greek Word-Makrothumia: long-passion, i.e. waiting sufficient time before expressing anger. This avoids the premature use of force (retribution) that rises out of improper anger (a personal reaction). Get the picture of (the patient restraint of anger – Longsuffering translated as forbearance and patience).

Paul is telling us to "PUT ON", i.e., dress for the day. We make a choice, we look in closet and choose an outfit to wear. Once you decide, you have to reach in the closet take clothes off the hanger and slip them on your body. Your clothes won't jump out of the closet and onto your body without your help; if you are going to wear them you have to put them on.

Paul is telling us that if we want to be loving, we must choose to "PUT ON" the Fruit of Spirit (longsuffering) and walk in it or you won't do it.

NOTE: To be loving, one must get pass themselves; do what's not considered the "Norm".

Norm is flowing in your flesh - jealous, boastful, arrogant, rude, selfish, irritable, resentful, rejoice when others are wronged, abusive, controlling and manipulative.

Abnormal is flowing in the Spirit - do not rejoice when others are wronged; be patient, kind, bear all things, believes all things, hopes all things, and endures all things

NOTE: You shouldn't love anyone so hard and deep. When the love they had for you changes and is over your

STUDY NOTES

STUDY NOTES

life is devastated. You should love yourself more than that. It doesn't matter how much you love them, it will not make them love you. (**That's TOXIC**)

Be loving but don't be a chump; be wise as serpents, etc., but speak truth to power.

The "Body of Christ" should be compassionate, sympathetic, merciful, and not cold hearted, non-judgmental, we are the soul saving station; not the throw people to the dog's station, those we consider misfits.

"LOVE'S IN NEED OF LOVE TODAY" -- DO I HAVE ANY TAKERS!

GOD SPEAKS WE LISTEN
Study Notes

_____
_____
_____
_____
_____
_____
_____
_____
_____
_____
_____
_____
_____
_____
_____
_____
_____
_____

'God Speaks, We Listen: A hermeneutic journey through the scriptures for spiritual growth and effective application.'

GOD SPEAKS WE LISTEN
Study Notes

'God Speaks, We Listen: A hermeneutic journey through the scriptures for spiritual growth and effective application.'

GOD SPEAKS WE LISTEN

Study Notes

_____

_____

_____

_____

_____

_____

_____

_____

_____

_____

_____

_____

_____

_____

_____

_____

_____

_____

'God Speaks, We Listen: A hermeneutic journey through the scriptures for spiritual growth and effective application.'

GOD SPEAKS WE LISTEN

Study Notes

_____
_____
_____
_____
_____
_____
_____
_____
_____
_____
_____
_____
_____
_____
_____
_____
_____
_____
_____

'God Speaks, We Listen: A hermeneutic journey through the scriptures for spiritual growth and effective application.'

GOD SPEAKS WE LISTEN

Study Notes

_____

_____

_____

_____

_____

_____

_____

_____

_____

_____

_____

_____

_____

_____

_____

_____

_____

_____

_____

'God Speaks, We Listen: A hermeneutic journey through the scriptures for spiritual growth and effective application.'

LESSON 10

GOD NEEDS YOU

LESSON 10

"GOD NEEDS YOU!"

SCRIPTURE: **Acts 17:22-28 (28a)**

TITLE: **God Needs You!**

SUBJECT: **God Needs You!**

PROPOSITION: I purpose to show the hearer that God needs us to be an extension of himself in the earth so others will know who he is.

OBJECTIVE: I want the hearer to be passionate about representing God and have compassion in all our efforts to be a soul winner.

We live in a world with millions of people; places to go, things to see. If you study the infrastructure of the various countries, you'll find it's a well-oiled machine so that each can flourish;

- Diversity of cultures.

- Splendor of the races

- Religion is sacred, various beliefs – believe in God, he's called by many names, different paths in pursuit of Him, or He's not believed in at all.

Paul visits Athens, the capitol city of ancient Greece:

- Centre of Greek art, architecture, literature and politics

STUDY NOTES

- Learning was stimulated and philosophers found Athens the place to be

- In the marketplace, you would see ancient Greek philosophers debate

Paul, a scholar himself, was taken aback by what he observed and it stirred his spirit (caused some major concern from a spiritual perspective):

The city was wholly given to idolatry.

There were more idols in Athens than there were in all of Greece.

Whatever strange gods were recommended to them they admitted them and allowed them a temple and altar.

The Athenians; intellectually stimulating – well learned and slaves to idols being deceived by Satan.

NOTE: Paul was pressed to engage in mental musing with some of the philosophers:

a. **Epicureans** – thought God was just like them; they denied God made the world or that He governs it; they indulged in the pleasures of senses and placed happiness in them.

b. **Stoics** - thought they were as good as God and in no way inferior to Him.

NOTE: In Paul's observation of idols; there was one that caught his attention with the inscription "To the Unknown God". Paul, a man of wisdom, seized the moment and poised the question to the philosophers. **"How is it that you live in a city that is, supposed to have a monopoly of wisdom; and the true God is an unknown God?"**

Paul preached Jesus Christ and His resurrection from the dead. Some mocked Paul, others wanted to hear more.

Paul wanted to show them that they had lost knowledge of the True God in their worship of the false gods they had made.

NOTE: We live in a day where one of the buzz words of the church is "Worshipper"

If you are a Satanic worshipper, you are opposed to any other power that is antagonistic to it.

If you are a God worshipper, you are opposed to any other power that is antagonistic to Him. If you don't see it this way, you believe in both "Powers".

NOTE: This brings to mind, one of the most powerful options we have in life: **The Ability to Choose!**

"SO" when it comes to who you worship:

You yield to the one based on your narcissistic mind-set so you can engage in your urges and appetites freely with no sense of accountability or standards – Satanic Worship.

> **"OR"**

You yield to the one that negated narcissism, defuses those urges and appetites; that causes you to submit and be accountable to a standard of righteous living – God Worship.

It would be presumptuous of me to think my life is in my own hands, but if God allowed me to be born:

- There is some life that must be lived.

- It also speaks to the fact there is a Source to my existence

- It's clear that if I am to exist, I must stay connected to the Source of my life.

NOTE: Might I add that there is never a disconnect, there may be some static in the hook-up, the reception is not always clear but if you get in the right spot, place or area the reception is restored.

NOTE: God loves us with an everlasting love (**II Corinthians 5:14**, "For the love of Christ constraineth us; because we thus judge, that if one died for all, then were all dead" – his love compels us back to the roots from which we came.

Whether or not we yield to it, again, it is our choice.

NOTE: Paul proceeded to tell them that; God made from one blood all men, one and the same nature that we might be engaged in mutual affection assistance toward one another.

OUR TIME IS IN HIS HANDS AND HE IS NOT FAR FROM US:

- In him we live – we depend on him and ought to live for Him.

- In him we move – our souls move our body – move toward Him.

- And have our being – propels us forward – consecrate our beings to Him.

NOTE:

- Don't know what the year holds.

- Don't know what will unfold.

- But I know that God is consistent:

  1. You can trust him – he's got your back.

  2. You're in him – he's the source of your supply.

  3. You depend on him – he never falls short of his word.

My brother, sister; young man and woman; boys and girls – GOD NEEDS YOU!!

NOTE: God created us for His purpose and saves us for His service to dispel the world's ignorance about Him and make Him known!

My brother, sister; young man and woman; boys and girls – GOD NEEDS YOU!

You must:

A. AMENABLE – ready to yield; submissive

B. ADHERE – to be devoted in allegiance; hearer but doer, etc.

C. ADAPT – to make suitable to conditions

   - Flexible – capable of being bent usually without breaking (Job – slay me, etc.)

   - Resilient – recovering readily from adversity (**Isaiah 43:2**)

   - Pliable – adjusting readily to change – SHIFT (**Jehoshaphat – II Chronicles 20**) (Car: the importance of shifting gears)

GOD SPEAKS WE LISTEN

Study Notes

_____

_____

_____

_____

_____

_____

_____

_____

_____

_____

_____

_____

_____

_____

_____

_____

_____

_____

_____

'God Speaks, We Listen: A hermeneutic journey through the scriptures for spiritual growth and effective application.'

GOD SPEAKS WE LISTEN
Study Notes

_____

_____

_____

_____

_____

_____

_____

_____

_____

_____

_____

_____

_____

_____

_____

_____

_____

_____

_____

'God Speaks, We Listen: A hermeneutic journey through the scriptures for spiritual growth and effective application.'

GOD SPEAKS
WE LISTEN

Study Notes

_____

_____

_____

_____

_____

_____

_____

_____

_____

_____

_____

_____

_____

_____

_____

_____

_____

_____

'God Speaks, We Listen: A hermeneutic journey through the scriptures for spiritual growth and effective application.'

GOD SPEAKS WE LISTEN

Study Notes

_____

_____

_____

_____

_____

_____

_____

_____

_____

_____

_____

_____

_____

_____

_____

_____

_____

_____

'God Speaks, We Listen: A hermeneutic journey through the scriptures for spiritual growth and effective application.'

GOD SPEAKS WE LISTEN

Study Notes

_____
_____
_____
_____
_____
_____
_____
_____
_____
_____
_____
_____
_____
_____
_____
_____
_____
_____
_____
_____

'God Speaks, We Listen: A hermeneutic journey through the scriptures for spiritual growth and effective application.'

LESSON 11

THE CLOSER I GET TO YOU

LESSON 11

"THE CLOSER I GET TO YOU!"

SCRIPTURE: **Joshua 22:1-5 (vs. 5)**

TITLE: **The Closer I Get to You!**

SUBJECT: **The Closer I Get to You!**

PROPOSITION: I purpose to show the hearer that an insatiable passion to cleave to God will cause us to be attentive to His voice, committed to be obedient to His word; carry out His great commission thus reaping His bountiful blessings.

OBJECTIVE: I want the hearer's pursuit of God to be there top priority which will subject everything we think, say, and do to be in line with God's mandate.

This text is the culmination of the faithfulness of God to His people but there are a few events that preceded it:

1. THE PROMISE - **Gen 13:12-16** – Lot and Abram separated. Abram lived in Canaan. God promised Abram a seed; all the land you see, north, south, east and west I will give to you and your seed forever.

2. THE REQUEST - Numbers 32:1-29- In route, in preparation to cross the Jordan - Moses summoned 12,000 soldiers to battle; to conquer the enemy. They won. When they returned the tribes of

Gad and Ruben requested of Moses and the high priest to take their residence East of the Jordan along with their families because they were herdsmen and the land was good for grazing - Moses honored their request - included the 1/2 tribe Manasseh, permitted them to build homes and stalls for their herds but;

3. The Prerequisite - before they could stay with their families and herds they had to go to battle with the remaining 9 1/2 tribes and help them conquer the land of Canaan. Moses made sure Joshua would see to it that the 2 1/2 tribes would honor their commitment.

4. The Mandate - to utterly destroy Canaan, every human being, animals, their altars, female goddess, burn graven images- this was a time period of 6-yrs. The Israelites Conquered Canaan!

5. The Promised Fulfilled- 9 1/2 tribes received the inheritance of the land West of Jordan and 2 1/2 (Gad/Rueben/Manasseh) received their inheritance East of the Jordan

WHICH BRINGS US TO THE TEXT: Joshua talking to people that have issues but they knew God and God knew them in an intimate way.

Joshua reminds the 2 1/2 tribes to take diligent heed to do the commandments/law as Moses charged them. The charge:

1. To Love God;

2. To Walk in His ways;

3.   To Keep his commandments;

4.   To Cleave to Him;

5.   To Serve him with all with all your might.

My emphasis is the 4th charge – TO CLEAVE TO HIM!

CLEAVE - cling to him; hold firmly to Him; embrace Him; cling to and unite with Him; to hold fast to Him; remain faithful to Him; stick to, stick with; stay close; stay with; keep close; follow closely.

NOTE: To cleave to someone, is this something we do automatically?

- Well for some of us this is a great challenge; we're hesitant - I'm being asked to give of myself, not sure I want to do that – have stipulations - what are the conditions? - Reservations - we are afraid; WHY DO THESE EMOTIONS COME UP?

Because some of the people we have allowed ourselves to get close have shattered our hopes; broken our hearts; crushed our dreams; are major disappointments and frustrate us to no end.

THIS IS A RISK I'M NOT SURE I WANT TO TAKE ANYMORE.

IN THIS TEXT:

We are commanded to Cling to God.

SOME MAY SAY - WHAT MAKES GOD A BETTER CHOICE? MOST OF THE PEOPLE THAT HAVE DAMAGED MY LIFE CLAIM THAT GOD IS THE CENTER OF THEIR LIFE.

STUDY NOTES

IN THIS TEXT:

We are commanded to Stay Close to God. Some may say Staying Close to God is too much pressure. His expectations are too high, it requires too much effort to walk the straight and narrow; it interferes with my plans. This whole God thing is foreign to me or I just don't get it!

BUT IN THIS TEXT:

We are commanded to Hold firmly to God.

PLEASE! I have better options with no pressure!

- I'll just take another hit - I feel euphoric;

- I'll take another drink- it mellows me out;

- I'll have an affair- and be stress free;

- I'll enjoy my pity party- all by myself

- I'll go on a shooting rampage-better them then me

- I'll continue to gamble the bill money away- I'm having fun

- My secrets will stay secrets- I got this

But the text said - Keep Close to God

This is not about doing it your way and putting God in it; it's about doing it God's way and you getting in it!

Let's consider 3-things that will encourage you to Cling to and unite with God. You need to know:

1. How God sees you. Apple of His eye; previous jewels – special, peculiar regal, royal sons and

daughters - heirs of His bounty.

GOD SEES YOU "HOLY" (Hebrew word "Kah-dosh")

- Set apart to Him and His purposes.

- Separation from everything profane and de-filing.

- Separated from and distinct from the world.

2. How God feels about you; you are always on his mind; He loves you with an everlasting love (**II Corinthians 5:14** "For the love of Jesus Christ compels us;" constrains us-a tight grip that pre-vents an escape) - you are the essence of Himself; He has plans for you; wants to prosper you not harm you; give you hope and a future; He will never leave you.

3. What God is bringing to the table is His sover-eignty (rules/reigns); His infiniteness (no limit to his being); His faithfulness (true to his word); His omnipotence (all powerful); His omniscience (all knowing); His omnipresence (everywhere same time); eternal (neither beginning or end); holiness (Supreme being without blemish or flaw); His justice (always does right); mercy (not getting from God what we do deserve); gracious (getting from God what we do not deserve); His love (he gives us blessings/happiness)

NOTE: The goal of this message is to show you that you can have a cohesive relationship with God. That's bound together with bonds that can't be broken.

WHAT IS THE KEY TO GETTING CLOSE TO God?

A. PURSUE GOD WITH PASSION

- Seek first the kingdom of God; Surrender your life to Him; Relinquish your will; Embrace His will; be Blessed (happy). He that hungers and thirst after righteousness will be filled.

- Draw nigh unto God, **Psalms 42:1**, "As the deer pants after the water brook, (pant means to long with intense eagerness) my soul after you oh God."

- Get rapped up, tied up, and tangled up in God's will so much so that His advice is sought concerning everything you do and every move you make.

- Pray-life; read, study the word; have personal worship; the fellowship corporately in worship.

- Be what He wants you to be, i.e., light in darkness, a witness; salt, influence.

- Do what He wants you to do (**Romans 12:1-2** present your body, be not conformed, to the world.)

- Our pursuit for God aligns our soul with the source from whence it came (We are dysfunctional-independent of Him, but totally in sync-dependent upon Him)

- Our pursuit for God arms our spirit to fight the battles with our flesh and deal with the vicissitudes of life.

What is the benefit of getting close to God?

B. THE CLOSER I GET TO GOD, HE MAKES HIM-
SELF KNOWN TO ME

- The closer I get to you, the more you make me see, by giving you all I've got your love has captured me.

- Low tolerance for sin, high tolerance for righteousness.

- Doesn't take cat naps nor does He sleep – He has an all seeing eye watching over His children. He's always available to you. He can't lie. Nothing is too hard for Him. He doesn't disappoint and He's reliable

- I am that I am - (Active present reality)

- Savior – Redeemer – Liberator – I will guide you – The source of your supply – Keeper ¬– Healer – Shield – Glory – the Lifter of you head.

- El Shaddai- more than enough

NOTE: If the "KEY" to getting close to God is pursuing Him with passion and the "BENEFIT" of getting close to God is He makes himself known to you; WHAT IS THE "WOW FACTOR" OF THIS CLOSENESS?

C. **GOD WILL BLOW YOUR MIND**

NOTE: It's said, trials come to make you strong but they also come to strip you; drain you; entrap you; distract you; slow walk you away from God.

STUDY NOTES

Sometimes we are victorious; sometimes we miss the mark; our inconsistencies will cause us to get into our feelings – doubt if we can do this thing or not.

- **Isaiah 43:18-19 (18**- Remember not the former things, neither consider the things of old) [Black & white TV to Color; Computers constantly updates] (19- I will do a "NEW" thing; I've already begun, don't you see it? I will make a way in the "Wilderness" (dry uncultivated land -waste) and rivers (water (rep's Holy Spirit, life, power sustenance) - in the desert.

- **I Corinthians 2:9**, "Eye has not seen, nor ear heard, neither has it entered into the hearts of man, the things which God has prepared for them that love him."

NOTE: God will blow your mind – will last pass this church experience. Think about it; talk about it; live it. Your faith will become your battle-ax, tearing down and disrupting whatever comes at you to tear you and God apart.

- Now unto Him that is able to do exceedingly, etc., Ephesians 3:20.

- Take a failure and give you success.

- Make something out of nothing.

- Make the impossible, possible.

- He'll make the doubters believers.

- He'll make those that hate you stepping stones to victory.

- He'll make Satan eat his words and prove him to be the liar that he is.

- His awesome ability will cause you to exuberate with crazy Praise.

SONG: TOTAL PRAISE

Lord, I will lift mine eyes to the hills

Knowing my help is coming from You

Your peace you give me in time of the storm

You are the source of my strength

You are the strength of my life

I lift my hands in total praise to you

GOD SPEAKS
WE LISTEN

Study Notes

'God Speaks, We Listen: A hermeneutic journey through the scriptures for spiritual growth and effective application.'

GOD SPEAKS WE LISTEN

Study Notes

_____

_____

_____

_____

_____

_____

_____

_____

_____

_____

_____

_____

_____

_____

_____

_____

_____

_____

_____

'God Speaks, We Listen: A hermeneutic journey through the scriptures for spiritual growth and effective application.'

GOD SPEAKS
WE LISTEN

Study Notes

_____

_____

_____

_____

_____

_____

_____

_____

_____

_____

_____

_____

_____

_____

_____

_____

_____

_____

_____

'God Speaks, We Listen: A hermeneutic journey through the scriptures for spiritual growth and effective application.'

GOD SPEAKS WE LISTEN

Study Notes

_____

_____

_____

_____

_____

_____

_____

_____

_____

_____

_____

_____

_____

_____

_____

_____

_____

_____

_____

'God Speaks, We Listen: A hermeneutic journey through the scriptures for spiritual growth and effective application.'

GOD SPEAKS
WE LISTEN

Study Notes

_____

_____

_____

_____

_____

_____

_____

_____

_____

_____

_____

_____

_____

_____

_____

_____

_____

'God Speaks, We Listen: A hermeneutic journey through the scriptures for spiritual growth and effective application.'

BIBLIOGRAPHY

The Interpreter's Bible Commentary

The New Interpreter's Bible Commentary

Halley's Bible Handbook

The Holman Illustrated Bible Dictionary

The Oxford Dictionary & Thesaurus

www. Dictionary.com

BIBLES:

The New International Version Study Bible

The New Living Translation

The Thompson Chain Reference Bible

The Message Bible

The Good News Bible

The Revised Standard Version

The Life Application Bible for Students

The Women's Study Bible

The Spirit Filled Life Bible

The Amplified Bible

ABOUT THE AUTHOR

Rev. Jackie Nelson is a native Washingtonian, born to Lena Branch and James Campbell. She was educated in the District of Columbia schools; a graduate of Cardoza High School. Rev. Nelson furthered her education at the Computer Learning Center where she majored in Programming and Operations. She received a Bachelor of Arts Degree in Religious Education and her Master of Divinity from Faith Christian University & Schools, and has certification as a Counselor through The American Association of Christian Counselors.

Rev. Nelson is the mother of two daughters, Charlene and Charrisse, and one son, Neal, who has gone on to be with the Lord. One of her greatest joys was to record an album with her children and travel throughout the United States as they ministered in song. She is also the proud grandmother of her dearly beloved grandchildren, E'manuel and Zari-Alexander. In June 2003, Rev. Nelson celebrated the release of her critically acclaimed solo project, "Jewels for You to Treasure."

At the tender age of 16, God spoke to Rev. Nelson and told her she was going to preach. She heard the Lord but did not take Him seriously, she laughed. Like Apostle Paul, Rev. Nelson discovered she could not fight against His will. It got to the point in her life that the call to preach God's Word became overwhelming and she had to be obedient to God and answer YES! In July 1989, Rev. Nelson preached her initial sermon and on November 30, 1991, she was ordained at Union Temple Baptist Church where she serves as an associate minister under the extraordinary leadership of Pastors Willie F. and Mary L. Wilson.

In her tenure of walking with the Lord, Rev. Nelson has worked as a choir president, missionary and deaconess; within her 1st 20 years of Christian service. As a contributing member of Union Temple, Rev. Nelson has served as a former directress of the UT Concert Choir, a mentor at the Adero House, a residential treatment center for Adolescent substance abusers, and as a committee member (emeritus) of Union Temple Womanhood Training program. She has also worked as Professor of Theology at National Bible College & Seminary at the National Church of God in Fort Washington, Maryland for over seven years.

She currently works with the Homeless and Ubuntu ministries respectively, (which represents 'Caring for God's People; God's Way'). Rev. Nelson is an anointed and dedicated instructor of the Leon Wright Seminary where she challenges God's people to give Him their all.

As the visionary of FULL CIRCLE MINISTRIES, Rev. Nelson is on a worldwide mission to win the lost at any cost because she knows the devil is on a 'diligent pursuit to destroy the souls of mankind.' This woman of excellence fervently desires that every individual encompass every aspect of life according to God's predestined purpose. To further incite this goal, Rev. Nelson is grateful for the January 2017 release of her book and curriculum: 'God Speaks, We Listen – a hermeneutic journey through the scriptures for spiritual growth and effective application.'

Her passions are her family, singing, working with the youth and elderly. Rev. Nelson's motto is, *"The heart of true ministry is to love Mankind with no restraint."*

www.ingramcontent.com/pod-product-compliance
Lightning Source LLC
Chambersburg PA
CBHW080504110426
42742CB00017B/2989